AUTHENTICITY REAWAKENED

The Path to OWNING Your Life's Story and
Fulfilling Your Purpose

VICKI ZNAVOR

AUTHENTICITY REAWAKENED

The Path to OWNING Your Life's Story and Fulfilling Your Purpose by
Vicki Znavor

Print: 978-1-944027-34-6

eBook: 978-1-944027-35-3

AUTHENTICITY REAWAKENED

To those who work with heart,
please know it matters.

CONTENTS

4: ARE YOU AUTHENTIC AT WORK?   67

5: AUTHENTICITY BASICS   95

6: CONFLICT, COURAGE, CURIOSITY, AND COMPASSION   119

7: WHAT YOU STAND FOR AND WHY YOU'RE HERE   143

1 CONNECTING THE DOTS

> *Your time is limited, so don't waste it living someone else's life. Don't be trapped by dogma which is living with the results of other people's thinking. Don't let the noise of other's opinions drown out your own inner voice. And most important, have the courage to follow your heart and intuition. They somehow already know what you truly want to become. Everything else is secondary.*[1]
>
> *—Steve Jobs*

If I were giving advice to those I love most in the world, I'd start with the words above. I'd like to start my relationship with you this way as well, but with two changes. First, I'd never use the word "dogma" and second, I will tell you that everything else can't be secondary. Values matter. They're not secondary. We're going to talk about values a lot in our time together because they will guide you on your path to authenticity.

Because you're reading this book, being authentic must be important to you. It should be. You're on this planet for a reason. It's your life's work to understand your purpose and the values that will guide you along the way, and to show up at work and in life as authentically as possible. It's my life's work to help you. This book will help you discover the following:

- Your pivotal moments
- Your values
- Your purpose
- How to speak up for what you want
- How to bring as much of your authentic self to work and life as you want

Everything delivered in this book will help you know your truth. When you know your truth, you are more confident and resolute in your decisions and relationships.

Despite all his achievements, Steve Jobs lived a life of contradiction and that must have caused him great personal angst. I can't help but wonder if this was because his values earlier in life were seemingly solely focused on achievement. While he drove his vision for Apple with unimaginable intensity, he was cruel to some of the very employees who developed its products. He studied Zen Buddhism but didn't achieve internal peace. He talked about having a beautiful family in the speech, but spent years denying paternity of his first child. It's also been said that "he was capable of great kindness and genuine compassion, and he was an attentive and loving father."[2]

When he spoke to the 2005 graduating class of Stanford University, he had been working for over thirty years, had been through tremendous highs and lows, and had been diagnosed with pancreatic cancer. He was a softer, gentler version of himself and he wanted to tell his story by way of three pivotal moments and the lessons he learned as a result. He kept it simple, but as was true for everything else he did, those words left a lasting impression.

I want to walk through the pivotal moments that he shared. As you listen to the stories, stop, and think about some of your own pivotal moments. We will walk through those moments together and they'll serve as the basis for identifying your personal values.

Dropping Out and Dropping In

Jobs's first story was about dropping out of college, an interesting choice for a speech to college graduates, but one that perfectly conveyed that there are many paths to success. He knew within the first six months of starting college that a traditional degree wasn't something he valued. He also cared about his parents and knew that his tuition was far too expensive for them. Like a lot of young people, Jobs didn't know what he wanted, but he was compelled to trust that things would work out. Rather than taking required courses, he opted to drop in on courses that interested him such as calligraphy. His face still lit up all those years later when he spoke about his fascination with this art form.

I'm sure his decision to drop out of school caused his parents and friends to wonder what in the heck he was thinking. But taking a calligraphy class? That probably seemed like a colossal waste of time for an obvious genius. Nonetheless, he followed his gut and ten years later he applied what he learned in that class to the creation of the typefaces and fonts found in the Mac. Looking back, the decision to drop out of school was the right decision for him.

Everyone's path is different. Dropping out of school would've been a horrible decision for me. It took me fifteen years of night school to get an undergraduate degree and three more for an MBA. During those years I had small children and worked full time, but it was something I had to do. My parents and husband knew how much it meant to me and I'm forever grateful that they did everything possible to help me achieve my dream.

What I know looking back is that had I not finished school, I wouldn't have been able to do the work that filled my heart with joy for forty years.

Love and Loss

Jobs's second story centered on being publicly fired from the company he created. While this was a painful and humiliating experience for him, he made a conscientious decision to keep doing the kind of work that he loved even if he couldn't do it at Apple. He went on to create NeXT and PIXAR. He also met his wife during that time. When Apple acquired NeXT, he returned to Apple, this time better equipped to lead because of his experiences at NeXT and PIXAR. He wouldn't have had those experiences without being fired.

During the speech he said, "sometimes life is gonna hit you in the head with a brick, don't lose faith." He spoke passionately about the fact that what kept him going during this difficult time was that he loved what he did.

I used to have a sign in my office that read "Do What You Love." Jobs's explanation for why this is important is outstanding:

Your work is going to fill a large part of your life and the only way to be truly satisfied is to do what you believe is great work. And the only way to do great work is to love what you do. If you haven't found it yet, keep looking and don't settle. As with all matters of the heart, you'll know when you find it.

Looking back, he could see that being fired was a blessing. I'm going to put my HR hat on for a moment and tell you this: Most people who lose their jobs for reasons beyond their control, realize that being fired nudged them to work that was much more fulfilling. I'm not saying that getting fired is easy; it stinks. But if you're ever fired, please know that something better usually happens as a result.

Death

His third story was about death. This story was made more profound because by this time his appearance reflected his health struggles. He said the following:

When I was seventeen, I read a quote that went something like "if you live each day as if it were your last, someday you'll most certainly be right." It made an impression on me and since then for the past thirty-three years I've looked in the mirror every morning and asked myself 'if today were the last day of my life, would I want to do what I am about to do today?' And whenever the answer has been "no" for too many days in a row, I know I need to change something.

YES!!! Life is short and if the place where you spend most of your time sucks the life out of your soul, get the heck out of there. Really—this is your life we're talking about here! In this book, we will cover how to know for sure if you dread going to work and what to do about it.

The thought of death is sad, but it can be an important reminder to us that our time on earth is limited and we don't get a lot of do-overs. When I was younger, I found it helpful to slow down and ask myself if one decision versus another could be a "deathbed" regret. Most decisions aren't deathbed decisions, but you'll encounter a few in your life.

For example, I always worked a full-time job when my kids were growing up. While I had no choice but to return to work with my first two, I had a choice with my third. Before making my decision, I thought about whether returning to work could be a deathbed regret. After a lot of gut-wrenching thought, I realized that I would regret *not* returning to work because I was a happier person when I was working. My daughters who were ten and six at the time were used to me working, so when I asked them if they wanted me to stay home, they said "Noooooooo!" I think they anticipated that I'd turn into a cleaning freak and this would change the quality of their lives as well. Good call girls!

This is a very personal decision for parents, but it was best for me and my family to keep working. This also meant that I would need to work hard to be the best mom that I could be. Returning to work will not be a deathbed regret.

Authenticity Reawakened

You might be thinking, "Well, most of us aren't Steve Jobs!" You're right, but your stories and purpose are no less important. You are here for a reason. There's no more important priority than to figure out what that purpose is and then take specific action to live up to it over time.

We reawaken our authenticity by making our values and purpose a priority repeatedly in our lives.

In early 2020, my heart told me that I needed to take a break, stop running on what felt like a hamster wheel and connect the dots of my life. What did it all mean? What does the next set of dots look like? Regardless of where you are in your career and life, it's good to take stock of where you are, who you are and what matters most.

As I took stock, I could no longer say that I loved what I did anymore. It hurts me to say that because I used to wake up every day and think that I was the luckiest person on the planet to do what I was doing. Seriously, I used to smile so big when describing my job that my face hurt. But things change. My heart knew that it was time to do something else and it was time to listen.

The universe started presenting things to me that I felt I should do, but I didn't understand *why*. I took a course before leaving my job and the first assignment was to identify my superpower. Despite thinking that the assignment seemed silly, I followed the instructions and asked friends and colleagues what they thought my superpower was – what did they think I did that seemed exceptional or a hallmark of my "being." It was "authenticity." They appreciated that I was myself and that I encouraged them to be themselves as well. My first thought was "is that really a superpower?"

Next, I saw a post on LinkedIn congratulating a man I met at an event. Gregg Lunceford wrote a book called *Exit From Work*. I sent him a congratulatory note and asked if he could talk. He was very generous with his time and shared what he learned from writing his book. He raved about working with his editor/publisher because she coached him throughout the process of writing. I thought, "OK good to know."

A few days later I went to the dentist. For some reason I felt strongly that I should mention book-writing to her. I thought to myself, "Why would my dentist need to know this?" but I went ahead and shared that I was curious about writing a book. She became highly animated, a huge smile crossed her face and said she had a friend who did amazing work with authors and she would introduce me to her.

On the way home from that appointment I realized that both people were talking about the *same* person: Melissa Wilson. Chicago is a big city and all of these "coincidences" were weird. The universe works in mysterious ways and I could feel it working to help me.

During my first conversation with Melissa she asked me to "find my superpower." What? I told Melissa that I already knew it because of the work I had recently completed. We agreed that I should consider writing about authenticity since that's something I knew so much about. Or did I?

Remember how Steve Jobs talked about listening to your gut? I believe that God (or the universe if you prefer) nudges us all the time. My natural inclination after leaving my job was to go out and get another job and do what I've always done. This time, everyone who cares about me said, "No!!! DO NOT DO THAT!" And that's what my heart was saying as well.

After deciding to listen to the voice inside, I embarked on the process of writing a book. I didn't pick the topic of authenticity—it picked me. What I know now is that so much of my purpose came about through my job, but that's not the only way to bring it to life.

My Promise to You

The book you hold in your hands is the result of countless hours of research, a review of hundreds of articles, many books, and my own personal experiences including over twenty-five years in human resources.

I've included stories, easy-to-understand examples, exercises, and tools you can use immediately. When you know your story, your values, and your purpose, you will be empowered to bring your authentic self to work and life in the way that you wish.

Here's what you'll find in this book:

- **Research about authenticity and behaviors that convey it.** You'll hear the story of Matt, who gave the impression of being authentic, yet he was far from it. You'll also hear about Tom Magliozzi, who was incredibly authentic and lived the life of his dreams.

- **Ways to be authentic at work and why it matters.** I share the stories about Rhonda and Leo, calling out specific behaviors and actions they took that conveyed authenticity as well as those where they fell short. You'll also learn about the risks associated with being authentic.

- **How to build your legacy.** Did you know that you're building a legacy? I share stories about Jessica Simpson and Brian Floriani and their paths to purpose. Floriani's message about going from success to significance is powerful.

- **What to do if you dread going to work.** I've provided you with several stories and examples that help you understand reasons for dreading work. There's an exercise that helps you to better understand why you dread going to work and what to do about it.

- **How to understand and tackle fear.** We're all afraid of something, but it's possible to manage fear. We'll look at a variety of fears you may experience at work. I share stories about Paula and Anna, who are both exceptionally talented, but they experience fears such as the fear of being thought incompetent or fired and the fear of being vulnerable. There's an exercise that I've used with others and re-tested recently that will help you understand fear and what you can do to manage it.

- **Basic steps to increase your authenticity at work.** I introduce you to behaviors you can put into action immediately. You'll also learn how to use the 5 Whys and a tool I created called the PIN Discussion Model to help you describe your concerns and ask for what you need in a straight-forward and simple way.

- **How to understand and handle conflict.** You'll learn about different conflict styles and how to use the Intentional Compassionate Conflict Model I created to help you address conflict with anyone.

- **How to discover your five pivotal life moments.** Your pivotal moments have influenced who you've become. I've shared my pivotal moments and included an exercise to help you understand yours.

- **How to discover your values.** It's incredibly important to understand your values because they will guide you throughout your life. I've shared my values and provided you with an easy-to-complete exercise that helps you identify yours.

- **How to discover your purpose.** I share my purpose and provide you with a three-step process to find yours. Your purpose will evolve as you grow and develop. This process can be used repeatedly in your life.

- **How to make the decision to stay in your job or leave your job.** There's an exercise to help you make this important decision.

- **How to plan your next steps.** I provide you with an easy-to-use action plan so you can plan your next steps and hold yourself accountable for completing them.

You're going to grow and change throughout your life. The more you practice following your gut and your authenticity, the easier it becomes to reawaken throughout your life. I've learned with you as I wrote this book. I hope that you enjoy it; I loved writing it.

2 AUTHENTICITY: THE BACKSTORY

> *I was once afraid of people saying, "Who does she think she is?" Now I have the courage to stand and say, "This is who I am."* [3]
>
> —*Oprah Winfrey*

What does it mean to be authentic? It turns out that after reading countless articles, books, and academic journals, I've learned there is no definitive definition of the term that thought leaders have agreed upon for this very important word, a word that seems to mean so much to us because we look for authenticity in others and they look for it in us.

A recent Google search resulted in 157 million references to authenticity. The Stanford Encyclopedia of Philosophy, for example, says it is the subject of many rich philosophical debates. Wikipedia states, "Authenticity is the degree to which an individual's actions are congruent with their beliefs and desires, despite external pressures." No wonder we're confused!

In this chapter we'll learn a bit about authenticity from an academic perspective as well as some relatable stories and examples.

The History of Authenticity

The concept of authenticity has been around for centuries. "Know thyself" is one of the maxims inscribed on the Temple of Apollo at Delphi, dating back to the fourth century BCE.

Most of us have heard or said the phrase, "To thine own self be true." In *Hamlet,* Polonius offers this advice to his son, Laertes, who is leaving to go to Paris. What's ironic about this is that Polonius was not someone who was self-aware. It's the classic case of "do as I say, not as I do" and without a doubt we see this double standard in our lives starting as toddlers.

In 2019, Yale professor Balázs Kovács found that there are fifteen independent subsets to authenticity. He warned researchers that "they'll miss the boat if they define authenticity in terms of two to four criteria and proceed on that basis."[4]

I agree with him completely. Human behavior is complex to say the least.

Who Am I?

Each of us must answer this question for ourselves. Sometimes we truly know the answer and sometimes we don't. The way I've often experienced this question most profoundly is by looking in the mirror. I don't mean the normal kind of looking in the mirror where you're just checking out your appearance. I mean looking directly into the eyes staring back at you and asking yourself "who am I?" and then standing there long enough to *feel* the answer. Go ahead—try it.

If the person looking back at you feels like a stranger or is someone whom you haven't connected with in a while, this is a clear sign that it's time to get back in touch with yourself. This book will help.

If, on the other hand, you know with certainty the answer to the question "who am I?" then that's terrific. Your answer today will not be the same ten years from now, so it's important to stay in touch with who you are.

The reality is that while it's a seemingly easy question to ask, it can take a lifetime to answer. Why? Because at its core it represents why we were put on this earth, our purpose, our reason for being.

Take David Viscott, who learned through his own life experiences that, as he put it, "The purpose of life is to discover your gift. The work of life is to develop it. The meaning of life is to give your gift away."[5] The quote is so inspirational that I wanted to learn more about the man who said it. As is true for most things in life, he was a lot more interesting than I expected.

In addition to being an author, Viscott was a psychiatrist who gave advice on a radio show called "Talk with Dr. Viscott" in the 1980s and 1990s. When a listener called in, he'd "coddle you, coaxing out the most intimate details—and then clobber you."[6] I've listened to a number of his radio shows on YouTube and this is a pretty good description of his approach.

At the end of his life, it became clear that he was not the man so many believed and trusted him to be. He had a larger than life ego, marital discord, and strained relationships with his loved ones. He died at the age of fifty-eight, reportedly deeply in debt.

Without a doubt, Viscott wasn't authentic in every aspect of his life, but nonetheless he made a positive and lingering contribution to the world. He wrote several books, took care of his ample patient load, lectured widely, helped many people solve their problems, and mentored many students, igniting their passion for psychiatry. But Viscott's journey was authentic. He wasn't striving for perfection, but rather spent his time studying and sharing his craft in the hope of helping others. In other words, he lived by the quote I shared. It's one I hope to live by and perhaps you do as well.

My first thought when I learned about Viscott was that his story seemed ironic in the same way as Polonius's advice to Laertes. But it's another reminder that there's no such thing as a perfect person. Like Viscott, we all make mistakes. Sometimes we may do something that's against our values and it brings pain to ourselves or others. This happens to everyone and, when it does, you must understand where you lost your way, get help if you need it, make amends, and move forward.

The journey to a purpose-driven life and career is comprised of thousands of moments. Some moments barely capture our attention, while others shake us to our core, calling into question our purpose, our values, and our beliefs. Those moments help us become who we're meant to be, but only if we learn from them.

Some of the most challenging choices that we can face are positive yet have the potential to negatively impact your life. For example, maybe you'll have an opportunity to assume more responsibility and make more money at work, but your new responsibilities will negatively impact aspects of your life that matter most. It's at these times when you must decide who you are and what matters to you or risk losing your way. Maybe Viscott lost his way and died before he could get back on track. I have no way of knowing.

As it relates to my own career, I'd like to think that, for the most part, I've spent forty years following Viscott's advice in terms of finding and strengthening my gifts although it sure wasn't a predictable or linear path. What I've learned in forty years is that our career paths are often filled with twists and turns, but many of these detours lead us to better paths than we could've anticipated or hoped for.

When I was just starting out, I made plenty of mistakes, was a jerk on occasion, tolerated some jerks that didn't deserve to be tolerated, and sometimes got lost in striving to climb the corporate ladder. Luckily, I always felt terrible when I treated someone poorly so that was never the norm for me.

I learned from all those experiences, but while I was experiencing them, I had no idea that I needed them to learn and grow. Everything that I've experienced in my life and work has made me, *me*.

I worked my way up from the most junior level to the C-suite but not in the typical way. I went to night school and it took me fifteen years to get my undergraduate degree and another three for an MBA. During most of this time I had young children at home, and it was a stressful time to say the least. I was striving to be a great wife, mother, employee, and student all at once. To say that I lost myself during that time is an understatement.

My life experiences, however, have contributed greatly to my career success. For example, my latest position was that of a chief human resources officer. In that position it was vitally important that I understand the challenges that people face in managing life and work.

While I couldn't have known it as a child, I learned important lessons early in my life that would help me become a thoughtful HR executive. My family often struggled to make ends meet, including not always knowing where the next meal would come from. I saw firsthand how frightened my parents became when one of them would get laid off from work. As an executive, I didn't want employees' children worrying the way that I did as a child.

While I'm proud of my career, I am most proud that I had the courage to be *me* at work. I wanted to show up each day as a genuine human being. More importantly, I wanted and needed others to bring their authentic selves to work as well because when they did, not only did our company greatly benefit, but it was a lot more fun than it would've been otherwise.

Behaviors That Convey Authenticity

> *I realized I was more convincing to myself and to the people who were listening when I actually said what I thought versus what I thought people wanted to hear me say.*[7]
>
> —*Ursula Burns*

While there's no set definition of authenticity, researchers have identified some behaviors that convey it and that's a good place to start in our quest to learn more. We'll look closely at each set of behaviors in this chapter to gain a deeper understanding of them. I've included quite a bit of research data but have supplemented it with actual work stories to help you understand the concepts.

- Being sincere and honest
- Being yourself
- Acting extroverted
- Being perceived as authentic
- Standing up for your beliefs
- Feeling that you're authentic

Being Sincere and Honest

If you're sincere and honest, you're well on your way to being perceived as authentic. Kovács found in his work that the words most often used to describe authenticity in people were the following: "honest, real, genuine, kind, trustful and sincere."[8]

Being sincere and honest is something that reasonable people aspire to be, but it's not easy to do on a consistent basis. Why? Because sometimes we realize that telling some-one the truth may be hurtful – either to others or to ourselves. Humans are wired to seek pleasure and avoid pain and telling the truth can be painful to say the least.

But what about the people who do demonstrate honesty and sincerity on a consistent basis? Believe it or not, sometimes people wonder what they're up to and they don't trust them.

On the other hand, have you ever known someone who was so agreeable that people thought they were insincere? Of course! It's hard to agree with everything.

Can someone be "sincere" if they're disagreeable or challenge a position? Absolutely! In fact, I usually feel that people who disagree are more sincere because they're willing to put themselves out there and tell you what they really think. Whenever I've been undecided about a decision, my go-to people are the people who I know will challenge my thinking, not the people who will agree with everything I say. Not everyone feels this way.

I once attended a meeting with several Human Resources leaders who were discussing behaviors that leaders in the organization should demonstrate to lead most effectively. One of the behaviors that they hoped to define was "authenticity." When the discussion centered in on the "kinds" of people that are or aren't authentic, it became clear that they felt that honest, nice, agreeable people were authentic, whereas people who weren't as nice or were more assertive were deemed *less* authentic.

I was genuinely interested in the discussion and asked, "Is it possible that someone who is less agreeable is actually quite sincere and authentic, but you don't like what they say or how they say it?" It seemed to me like a reasonable question, but I noticed that some of the people looked at their buddies across the table and gave the look that conveyed to me, "Ugh, what is she talking about?!" The response was, "Well, I don't think that every behavior has to be thoroughly defined."

I thought that every behavior should be defined because when people are deciding how others will be evaluated at work, they should understand what's expected of them. With that in mind, I responded by saying so. My commentary was met with silence, I got a look that made me feel that I had three eyeballs, and the discussion moved on to defining the next behavior. My thoughts and my input weren't appreciated.

I replayed that discussion over and over in my head. Here's why: in that moment, I understood without a doubt why I didn't fit in with this group and likely never would. Their response to my comments conveyed "your thoughts really don't matter." That was interesting to me because I had studied the topic for years and I knew what I was talking about.

I'd seen many of these same people give speeches about inclusion, yet they weren't interested in opinions that differed from their own. The irony wasn't lost on me and I believe this is one of the greatest challenges we have in building truly inclusive organizations. Maybe I'll cover that in another book.

Anyway, that team probably thought I was closer to being a pain in the butt than I was to being sincere and honest. And you know what? I can be both, which was actually the point.

The reason I shared this story is to help you see that being sincere and honest isn't easy because some people, including some leaders, only want you to agree with them.

In my case, I wouldn't have been my authentic self if I sat there and not done my best to contribute to helping the team. You're going to be faced with these kinds of challenges too and you're going to have to decide whether it's worth it to speak up.

Being Yourself

> *The people who seem comfortable in their own skin and who are bringing their real selves to work generally are also the same people who can have an honest dialogue with their bosses, who have the courage to ask for the promotion, the bonus, or the new assignment, and who are quick to point out when someone or something is impeding their success.*[9]
>
> — *Carla Harris*

If you're not familiar with Carla Harris, please check out her videos on YouTube. She is the Vice Chairman, Managing Director and Senior Client Advisor at Morgan Stanley. She's a black woman working on Wall Street who rightfully takes great pride in being herself. She's been recognized countless times for her strong leadership, has written books and often shares lessons which she calls "Carla's Pearls". These are the lessons she's learned over the years that will help others in their career pursuits.

Being yourself takes courage. Have you ever been encouraged to "just be yourself," but when you said what you really thought, you were told that it would've been better to say such and such "this way" rather than the authentic way you expressed it?

In other words, be yourself—but not really. This leaves many of us to wonder if the encouragement to "just be yourself" is something others feel they're supposed to say but they actually mean "be more like me." When people give you advice, they usually have good intentions, but sometimes it comes out the wrong way and it's confusing. Have you experienced this yet?

There are many ways that being yourself at work shows up. It can be in how you dress, whether you're comfortable saying that you need time off to attend events that are important to you, how you speak, wear your hair and on and on.

I have a friend Rhonda who has a bigger than life personality. She's a magnificent leader and someone I admire more than words can say. She used to open her presentations with a few slides about her family because she wanted her colleagues to know her and what was important to her. She also shared information in a clear, concise way rather than using a bunch of corporate-speak. She was willing to be herself and she let everyone else know that they could be themselves with her as well.

I spent a lot of years early in my career trying to say things the "right" way rather than the way that I would ordinarily say them. What a waste of time! What I know now is that any attempts to be anyone other than who I really am is wasted time and energy. The same is true for you.

To be yourself, you need to be a bit like my friend Rhonda and have a strong sense of who you truly are. Researcher Grace Rivera and her colleagues argue that while it may be difficult if not impossible to know one's true self, just feeling that your actions are guided by your true self leads to personal meaning and satisfaction.[10] In other words, being your authentic self is good for you!

Let's go back to the research for a bit. As it relates to being ourself, apparently the research indicates that the self in fact consists of *many* selves depending on situational context. In other words, you show up differently in different situations.

"For Joseph, his CEO self is activated at work, leading him to view and judge himself in line with the characteristics and opinions he associates with himself as CEO."[11] So Joseph is the CEO at work and he acts that way, but when he goes home he likely acts very differently. I've known several spouses of executives who rule the roost at home, so this research makes sense to me.

I don't think one can be considered authentic if your personality changes dramatically between work and home.

Other researchers, including Roy Baumeister, say that you can't have multiple selves, but you can have multiple concepts of self and these are different versions of the same self.[12]

Is it better to show up as many selves, or oneself? I have these visions of what I imagine as different shirts with logos that get changed given a particular situation. Geez, that's just too complicated for most of us, isn't it?

And lastly, believe it or not, people tend to see some aspects of their behaviors as who they truly are, while other behaviors aren't viewed that way. What they mean is that if we do something that we feel is representative of who we truly are, then we accept that as part of our authenticity.

On the other hand, if we do something that seems to be against our general nature, we say that we weren't being ourselves. I've done this before, how about you? The researchers say (and I agree with them) that everything you do is representative of your authentic self – even the things you aren't so proud of doing.

Acting Extroverted

> *To succeed in life, you need three things: a wishbone, a backbone and a funny bone.*[13]
>
> —*Reba McEntire*

We all like attention and extroverts are great at getting it. Unfortunately, introverts may sometimes be passed over simply because they didn't speak up.

One of my daughters is an extreme introvert. She's not shy, but she doesn't feel like she has to say something unless it's necessary. She is highly intelligent, but when she was in school her teachers used to assume that because she wasn't talkative that she wasn't confident. I used to have to help her teachers understand that introversion doesn't mean you're not confident, it means that you don't get your energy from other people.

On the other hand, extroverts do get their energy from others. I've seen many extroverts who have learned early that they can talk their way out of most things. That's a great skill to have without a doubt, but it's not a substitute for doing your homework. Some of the extroverts I know have been given a lot of free passes because they engage people in conversation and seem more likable. Extroverts get the benefit of this bias when it comes to being thought of as authentic as well.

Rivera's research indicates that both extroverts and introverts feel more authentic when they're acting extroverted. Baumeister also mentions this finding and says, "It's an irksome finding for researchers that introverts feel more authentic when they're being extroverted." If they were being authentic, they'd feel more authentic when they're being introverted!

As an introvert myself, I agree that when you put yourself out there, even when it's uncomfortable, you may connect more deeply with others which may enable you to see aspects of your authentic self from a different perspective. Connecting with others feels good and that feeling can build your confidence to keep sharing more of yourself with others. It's like building muscle. If you're willing to put yourself out there a little bit at a time, you may find that it's not only easy, but it enhances your life. That's what happened to me.

Being Perceived as Authentic

Katrina Jongman-Sereno and Mark Leary have concluded that "the importance that people place on being authentic may arise from strong social pressures to be who and what one claims to be. To deal effectively with others, people need to know what other people are like, what motivates them, and whether they can be trusted."[14]

In addition, Baumeister says, "To spell it out, the troubling implication is that people associated authenticity with doing what society regards as good rather than with what their true inner nature dictates. Most of the data on authenticity seem to be infected with this confound."[15]

We've all heard the saying "perception is truth." The way I've seen this play out most at work is via the recency effect. What this means is that people tend to remember what you did most recently. So, if you're someone who consistently does great work, but a mistake is observed by a senior person, that might become their perception of you.

Conversely, I've seen people who have done mediocre work, but they've been observed by a senior person at the perfect moment and they are viewed favorably because of that one observation.

I wish that I could tell you this doesn't happen, but it does and it's a challenge to overcome. We'll talk more about mistakes later in the book, but the best way to handle a situation where you're a great performer but you made a mistake is to apologize, learn from it and continue to do your best work.

As for the mediocre performers who just got lucky, they eventually get found out, but sometimes it takes a while.

I once worked with a guy who I'll call Matt. We were both vice presidents in a large, global organization. Matt viewed himself as an honest, honorable person and certainly management did as well. He would speak at various employee events and always made a very favorable impression: he had technical expertise and came across as a humble, thoughtful, and authentic person. I shared this view as well.

Unfortunately, once I started working closely with Matt, a side of him that was never obvious in his public persona emerged. He would often confide in me and I found our conversations disturbing. The public Matt was not the Matt that I grew to know. He would criticize management and say that they didn't know what they were doing. He'd talk about his peers (he seemed to forget that I too was a peer) and others highlighting what he saw as their flaws and shortcomings.

One person, let's call him Donald, seemed to really ruffle Matt's feathers, and at the time I couldn't understand why. Matt would say things like, "Donald is nothing but an imposter." That struck me as ridiculous because Donald was and continues to be a noted expert in his field. Matt on the other hand seemed to spend most of his time at work talking about people and creating PowerPoint decks that were beautiful but mostly highlighted Matt's contributions. Matt was an expert at nothing more than tooting his own horn. You know someone like this don't you? Every organization has at least a few "Matts."

Matt consistently got more praise for his work than Donald, even though Donald was doing far superior work and was a role model for the company's values. By this point in my career I'd seen this kind of "fakery" countless times, and it infuriated me. I couldn't believe that no one saw Matt for what he was or, if they did, they didn't seem to care.

To my great surprise, I was told that Donald would be losing his job as part of a reduction in force and Matt was going to be my new boss. I was really angry about this; I felt that Matt had a smidgen of talent compared to Donald, behaved in a way that was completely inconsistent with the company's mission, vision, and values, and was himself the true imposter.

When I had my first meeting with Matt, now my new manager, I didn't hold back. I said to him, "I will continue to be professional and do everything I can to support you and the team to succeed, but I've seen you. I know what kind of person you are, and your behavior doesn't live up to what we profess is important to this company. I'm not going to be able to forget it and it's important that you know that."

There wasn't much he could say because he couldn't deny the terrible things that he said to me about others. I thought long and hard about whether I was going to say those words to him because I knew that by doing so, I was putting my career at risk. But, for the first time in my career, I knew that if I didn't say something, I'd forever be ashamed of myself. It was worth saying what I said to him no matter what happened as a result.

Matt and I worked together for a few years, but the next time that a reduction in force occurred, I told the company—one I had worked at for a very long time—that I would be happy to be added to the list. In retrospect, I just couldn't accept that Matt and others like him were valued so highly and it made me feel disgusted, sad, and disappointed. By the way, Donald went on to start his own company and has been wildly successful. Not sure what Matt is doing.

Company culture is an outcome of everything that happens in an organization. Seeing Matt and others like him disregard the values of the company yet rise through the ranks was a sign to me that the culture was changing in a way that was no longer consistent with my personal values. I had to leave the company. With the benefit of hindsight, it was a good decision on my part to leave and I never regretted doing so.

I've shared with you that experiences form who we become and what we value. The experience with Matt made me more aware of the kinds of things and people that erode company culture. I also learned that leaders often get blindsided by trusting their observations more than they should.

Matt was a phony. He portrayed himself as a humble, grateful guy to management and employees, but it didn't take a genius to see that all his presentations were basically about himself. Once they learned about Matt's true behavior, they had already invested in him as a leader, so they looked the other way.

There is no such thing as a perfect company culture. As you learn and grow your career, it will become important not only to do the work that you love, but to do it at a place that inspires you to be your very best. Culture matters.

Standing Up for Your Beliefs

> *Stand for something or you will fall for anything. Today's mighty oak is yesterday's nut that held its ground.*[16]
>
> —*Rosa Parks*

I love the quote above. It's so true, isn't it? It's difficult to stand up for everything, but by now you should know what things are so important to you that you will stand up for them. Take a moment to think about what those things are for you. What are the kinds of things that you'd stand up for even if you know that you'll be criticized for doing so?

If you saw someone being mistreated at work, would you say something? Would it matter if it were an executive who mistreated that person? If you were in a room with your friends at work and one of them used racial slurs that you hopefully found highly offensive, would you say something to them about it?

According to the researchers, standing up for your beliefs is being authentic, but some people confuse this behavior with integrity. It's not the same thing. For example, people who have a great deal of integrity may be authentic, but people who don't have much integrity may or may not be. This is perhaps determined by the extent to which they hide their behavior. Immoral people may be authentic, but they're obviously low in integrity.[17]

An executive I worked with, let's call him Tom, exemplified being congruent with beliefs and values. In other words, his behavior matched his words. He was known for saying things such as "It's all about the people" or "We bring in the best talent, set the bar really high, treat them well, and they'll deliver more than anyone can imagine." He said these things consistently, whether in front of employees, his team, the board of directors or with me behind closed doors.

He's earned the trust and deep respect of everyone who worked with him. He'll forever be my favorite boss and leader. He genuinely believed that people mattered and his actions supported his words.

Feeling That You're Authentic

Most of us think of ourselves as authentic, don't we? Jongman-Sereno and Leary found that people feel most authentic when they act extraverted, agreeable, conscientious, emotionally stable, and intellectual. [18]

If you think about the people you feel are authentic, they probably exhibit many of the traits described above. Can someone who is less agreeable be authentic as well? Yes, of course. Can someone who isn't "intellectual" be authentic? Yes! In fact, when people present information at work and they use a lot of technical terms or impressive-sounding words sometimes it's a sign that they don't know what they're talking about. I love it when people explain things using simple, easy-to-understand language.

We appreciate authenticity in others, especially at work, because sadly it's not the norm. Isn't it refreshing when someone's actions are consistently in alignment with their words? Do you find yourself disappointed, but often not surprised, when someone says one thing and does another?

Consider some of the ways that you can show up at work and just be yourself. Maybe it's as simple as writing in a style that is consistent with how you talk. Or perhaps it's making a commitment to yourself that the next time someone talks poorly about someone at work, you're going to share how you feel about that kind of behavior. Authenticity starts with small steps.

Reawakening your authenticity means committing to understanding your values repeatedly in your career and working in a way that's true to them. Whether others are authentic is out of your control. Whether you are authentic, on the other hand, is entirely within your control.

In an average career, you'll spend over 83,000 hours at work. That's such a long time, especially if you're doing work you don't like and showing up as someone else to do it.

I recently read the obituary for Tom Magliozzi, who hosted the *Car Talk* radio show with his brother Ray. Those two guys had the best time on their show, laughing nonstop. Despite my not caring anything about cars, I listened to their show all the time; it was both hilarious and incredibly informative. If you've never listened to one of their shows, look them up on YouTube. One of my favorite shows was when they invited Martha Stewart, but there is a huge selection to choose from.

Tom died in 2014. His obituary tells the story of how he came to work on the show:

In his late 20s, he was making his tedious 45-minute commute in traffic one morning, had a near miss with another car, and had a revelation that he was wasting his life. Upon arriving at work, he walked into his boss' office and quit on the spot. He hated putting on a suit and working in the 9-to-5 world. After a period spent happily as a Harvard Square bum, a house painter, an inventor, a successful PhD student, and an auto mechanic, *Car Talk* became his focus, and Tom spent the rest of his working life doing what he was born to do. Making friends, philosophizing, thinking out loud, solving people's problems, and laughing his butt off.[19]

I love that Tom found the work that mattered most to him and made him happy. His happiness had a multiplier effect: he made so many people happy each week, me included.

Throughout this book I will guide you in developing meaningful steps in your journey to an authentic, purpose-driven career. When you know yourself and your values, have confidence, and know what's important to achieve in your work, you will succeed. More importantly, you will know that you spent your life at work in a way that was fulfilling and meaningful to you.

The Journey Ahead

My goal with this book is to help you define your unique path to authenticity at work. I'm taking every step of the journey with you. Let's take a quick look at what's ahead:

- Chapter 3 describes authenticity and the ways it shows up as well as some common misconceptions about it. Authenticity isn't the same as transparency or being nice.

- Chapter 4 describes what you might be experiencing if you're not bringing your authentic self to work. We'll also touch on the elephant in the room: fear! We all have it and learning to manage it is key to success in most aspects of our lives.

- Chapter 5 highlights some basic principles of authenticity, along with some easy things you can do to quickly ignite your progress toward a more authentic you at work.

- Chapter 6 goes deep on the tough stuff: Conflict, courage, curiosity, and compassion.

- Chapter 7 provides you with all you need to understand the pivotal moments in your life, define your values and create your purpose statement.

- Chapter 8 helps you decide whether it's best to stay in or leave your current job.

- Chapter 9 discusses how letting go is the only way to move toward who you're meant to be in this life.

- Chapter 10 contains a list of 100 ways to demonstrate authenticity.

Each chapter will include key takeaways that you can put into action right away and build upon as we proceed through the book. I'm excited to work with you and I hope you're excited as well.

3 WHAT DOES IT MEAN TO BE AUTHENTIC AT WORK?

> *The privilege of a lifetime is to become who you truly are.*
> —*C. G. Jung*

The truth about authenticity is that it's not about someone else's perception of you. It's about knowing who you truly are and bringing as much of that person to work as possible in very deliberate ways.

In the previous chapter, I shared the behaviors that convey authenticity that research shows will give others the perception that one is authentic. I agree with the research, but if the goal is to truly *be* authentic at work, then it's not good enough to have some high-level description without understanding ways to bring it to life.

In an article in *O, The Oprah Magazine*, Tina Opie, PhD, an associate professor at Babson College, described what authenticity at work looks like for her:

> In my case, it might look like this: I would really like to raise my hand in a meeting because I have

something to say, and coming from me, a black Christian academic woman, it might be divergent from the other opinions being shared. But I do it anyway. It's what I want to do internally, and it's concordant with my external behavior.[20]

Opie is a highly accomplished woman whose research focuses primarily on how organizations can create workplaces that successfully leverage individual differences and convey respect for individual contributions.[21] The description she provided for the article is one way of many that she demonstrates her authenticity.

Opie described what authenticity means for her when she attends meetings. If she were leading rather than attending a meeting, she'd no doubt have a different description of how her authenticity would show up. I can imagine her saying that she'd engage the attendees by stating her position about the topic, describing her personal experience and being deliberate about hearing others' points of view because doing so matters to her.

Someone else would lead or attend meetings differently. Even those who have the same beliefs and values as Opie would show their authenticity differently because they're different people.

If I were to ask you what being "yourself" at work means to you, what would be your answer? Are there certain principles that you'd say would be obvious regardless of your role in the meeting?

For example, maybe you'd say that you like to show your appreciation for others. Do you do this? If not, what are some ways that you can start doing this going forward? One suggestion is that if someone has done something that you genuinely appreciate, you can send them a note to thank them or you can express your appreciation at a team meeting. Everyone likes to be appreciated so find ways that you can do this on a regular basis.

Maybe you are really focused on inclusion so how can you demonstrate this in your work? Perhaps if you are at a meeting and someone isn't saying much, you could ask that person if they'd like to add something to the discussion.

Another way to demonstrate authenticity at work is to be present. When someone is speaking with you or talking in a meeting, don't look at your phone. Put it away and listen. Treat your colleagues the way you want to be treated; it goes such a long way.

Some people might say (if they're being honest) that it's particularly important that they be viewed as the smartest or most senior person in the room. I'm not a fan of this behavior, but if it's important to them and you genuinely appreciate their contributions, then be sure to thank them for their great ideas.

I shared a few simple examples of ways you can be more authentic at work. Take a moment to think about how you like to be seen in typical work situations. Are you showing up this way now or are you hiding some aspects of yourself that prevent you from doing so? Decide on a few changes you can make going forward and then start practicing them right away.

My Early Work Years

> *Believe you can and you're halfway there.*[22]
> —*Theodore Roosevelt*

Many people aren't comfortable being authentic at work, especially early in their career. The start of my career can best be described as packing up the car and heading out on a trip with no idea where I was going, but I hoped it would be fun. I wasn't striving for authenticity; that wasn't even a consideration at the time. Nor did I have any idea what I wanted to or could become.

My only goal after graduating high school was to get a job that paid well enough so I could get an apartment and pay my rent. My expectations were basic because I wasn't taught to expect anything more from work other than a paycheck. No one in my life ever even mentioned that finding fulfilling work or an enjoyable workplace should be an aspiration.

When I was in high school, I took on leadership roles such as being the President of my class and captain of the cheerleading squad, but I was such an introvert! I didn't go to parties and in social settings, I was the girl who found one person to speak with the entire time. I'd describe myself the same today.

My teachers saw that I was intelligent, but their hopes for me included working at the local mill as either a scientist or a tour guide. I grew up in a factory town and our teachers worked hard to prepare us for careers in local industry, despite the fact that Chicago was less than thirty minutes away. While no other career choices were ever discussed with me, I knew that neither option seemed like a good fit.

As luck would have it, as I was nearing graduation, my best friend Rhonda's aunt asked her if she knew anyone who could use a job working in a small office in (almost) downtown Chicago. I'd make about $125 a week (no, that's not a typo!) and do general office work.

I was so excited to accept the job. Looking back, it was such an important step in my career journey and life. In that tiny little smoke-filled office (people could smoke at work back then), I learned about office politics, how important managing expenses is to a business and the pride that comes with doing the best work possible. I'm glad I started working at a small, family-owned business because I learned so many lessons that I used throughout my career from the sweet family for whom I worked.

In his book *Authentic: How to Be Yourself and Why It Matters*, Stephen Joseph writes:

> When we reflect on our past, we can see that the directions we have taken can often be traced back to one single, short moment. Our lives often turn on what at the time seem to be the most trivial of occurrences: a chance meeting and a single sentence that was or wasn't said. As one ages and becomes wiser, it becomes possible to see that life is governed in this way and that the big things in life, such as who one marries, what career one pursues, where one lives and so on, often arise from such unexpected every day and, at the time, seemingly trivial

encounters. To be able to navigate life successfully, so that you make the best decisions for yourself at any given moment, you need to be authentic—you need to be able to counter external influences pulling you to go against the grain of your own gut feelings.[23]

Looking back on that first job I can validate what Joseph says about a chance encounter changing your entire life. I was lucky that my friend recommended me for the job although I had no real experience. All I knew when I was starting out was that I loved office work such as typing, calculating (Excel didn't exist yet, so we used adding machines), sitting behind a desk, and working with people who could pass along some of their wisdom to me. I also knew that if I screwed up, I would be on my own; my parents wouldn't be able to rescue me. That was both a heavy load and a gift. I learned early on to own my successes and failures.

I stayed at the small company for a few years and then went to work for a major real estate firm where I stayed for a year or so. That was such a fascinating step for me because all the brokers were young, great looking, rich, and confident. Oh my. It was the early 1980s and I can still remember some very suggestive photos on their desks that wouldn't be allowed today, but it was a fun place to work.

My next position was as an entry-level administrative assistant at one of the largest companies in the US. I was twenty-one years old, had very good secretarial skills and a willingness to learn. I accepted the job because the company offered tuition reimbursement, a benefit that wasn't common at the time. This was the only way I could afford to take college courses.

At twenty-one I felt like an old lady. Most of my friends had gone away to college or were attending courses locally while living with their parents. They were going to parties and I was living on my own and working forty hours a week. The upside of this is that with the tuition reimbursement benefit, I could *finally* afford to take courses *and* pay my rent. Fortunately for me, I could take night classes within walking distance of my apartment. It was a dream come true.

While it wasn't a conventional way to go to college, it was a great way for "me" to go to college because so many wonderful things happened to me as a result. As it turns out, I met my husband in the very first class I took. Years later I am honored to sit on the Board of Trustees of that school, Calumet College of St. Joseph. I couldn't have known all this at the time; that's not how it works in life.

What I also didn't know at the time was that it would take fifteen years to get a degree and another three after that to earn an MBA. Had I known just how steep the hill I was climbing was, I would've said, "I CAN'T do this!" I might have given up before I even started. But I didn't.

I decided that I would stop thinking about the hill and just focus on each class as being one step closer to the goal. I'd say to myself, three credits down, x to go. When x was 141, I was overwhelmed. You know that feeling you get when you want to do something, but you know the odds are heavily stacked against you? Yeah, that's how I felt. On the outside I'd tell others how excited I was to be going to school, but there was a little voice that simultaneously told me that I'd never really finish.

I decided that if I paid too much attention to that little voice, I'd be toast. I decided the only way to finish would be to focus on how important it was to my life to get a degree. I knew that I was just as smart as anyone else and not having a degree was preventing me from being considered for jobs that I was more than capable of doing.

After a lot of thought, I concluded that in fifteen years I could be a person with a degree or one without one. I was determined to be a person with a degree if it killed me—and it almost did. Some things in life are worth giving your all and I was determined that I wasn't going to leave this earth without a degree. My sweet daughters used to ask me if I'd be the oldest college graduate ever and I answered honestly that it was quite possible. Humor helps.

I have passed along the advice that I gave myself way back then many times. When you want to do something, but it seems nearly impossible, imagine how you'll feel in the future if you don't achieve the goal. Time will keep passing no matter what. You get to decide what you will do as the time passes.

As I nudged closer to finishing school, I had three small children (our youngest was only one) and was working full-time. Sometimes I look back on that time and I wonder how in the world I was able to go to work, school, clean my house and care for the kids. I was blessed to have had a lot of support from my parents, husband and my boss at the time which made achieving my goal possible. I am forever grateful to my personal "village" for helping me achieve my dream.

I could see the finish line, but I still had a long way to go because I could only complete one or two classes each semester. I was also starting to hit my stride at work in terms of taking on more complex assignments and demonstrating strong leadership capabilities. I had heard the quote that you can have everything in life, but never at the same time. It's true. No matter what decision I made, either my family or my job would not get all of me, but I did the best I could to give as much of me as possible to all aspects of my life. Do you experience this as well?

Early Lessons

> *When you realize how much you're worth, you'll stop giving people discounts.*[24]
>
> —*Karen Salmansohn*

While I didn't yet have a degree, I had a lot of enthusiasm and my manager kept giving me challenging assignments. I was happy to do the work because I was learning, but I knew I was underpaid, and it was starting to frustrate me.

Particularly annoying to me was a guy in my department who oversold his skills in his interview by a long shot. He was making $40,000 a year more than what I was making but doing significantly less complex work. I remember being in meetings where our manager would hand out assignments. I'd have ten things and he'd have one or two and neither was the kind of work that someone at his level should be doing.

Up to this point, I had been passive about pay because I felt inferior about not having a degree. Once I gained confidence that my skills and contributions were worth more, I let my manager know how I felt about the situation. Talking to him about this was a huge step for me, but I was confident that I had every reason to be frustrated. He said, "Listen, there's a club and you get to be in it when you have a degree. Finish school. I'll support you in doing that, but you have to finish."

That answer rightfully wouldn't fly today, and I hated that conversation with every ounce of my being, but it made me more determined than ever to finish school. I knew that as soon as I finished, he would either pay me properly or I was out of there and he knew it as well. When I finished school, he paid me fairly and I stayed for quite some time after that discussion.

Here's what I learned: at the end of the day, it doesn't matter if you achieve your goal in four years or fifteen. I had a slow start—so what! If you have a goal, just ask yourself if achieving it—no matter how long it takes—is worth it to you. If it's worth it, just keep going. DO NOT GIVE UP! I'm glad I kept going. I'm proud that I finished and doing so provided me with opportunities I never would've had otherwise. The same can be true for you.

Are you holding on to a dream? If so, what will it take to make it come true? Start making a list of what you need to do to realize your dream and then create a plan for getting it done. If you have no idea how to proceed, talk to someone who has already achieved what you hope to achieve. People genuinely want to help people achieve their goals. Don't wait – take one step today to make it come true!

Another lesson I learned is that good advice doesn't always feel good in the moment. In fact, some of the best advice that you'll ever get will hurt. Whenever someone is willing to give you advice, be willing to accept it because it may be exactly what you need to move forward.

Back to the early days of my career. While I knew I was smart and capable of learning, I was acutely aware that there was much I didn't know. I had never seen college-educated businesspeople at work. I was in awe of their intelligence, confidence, work ethic, and lifestyle. I wanted to be like them, but never in my wildest dreams did I think I could or would reach their level in the organization. I focused on learning rather than attaining a specific level. This has always served me well.

My job was to type, file, and do secretarial work. I sat next to a nice older woman who was a terrific lifelong secretary. One day she saw me reading the mail and asked why I bothered. I told her I wanted to understand what was coming across the desk because that would help me learn. I hoped that I could take on more responsibility someday. She said, "You're wasting your time; you're never going to understand what that stuff means, and (cue eyeroll here) your job is to type."

While her words sounded harsh at the time, they weren't intended to be cruel. I think she felt that she was protecting me from extra work and from being disappointed in myself for not grasping the content. She may also have thought that the work I was learning to do was important and needed to be done so I shouldn't aspire to do anything else.

I kept reading the mail anyway, asked questions, supported the team, and became a go-to person. I stayed in the department for five years. By the time I left for a promotion elsewhere in the company, I was helping gather data for tax returns and had several other responsibilities that helped me succeed in subsequent roles.

Because I did more than was expected of me and had a good attitude, the senior members of the team helped me even when doing so meant that I would leave their department. Nearly forty years later, some of the people I worked with then are people I admire and care about deeply. I was blessed that they were such an important part of my career.

Behaviors and Actions That Convey Authenticity

Let's take a look at a few of the **Behaviors and Actions That Convey Authenticity** from Chapter 1 and the ways that I demonstrated those behaviors early in my career. My goal is to walk through stories, show you the behaviors and some actions that convey authenticity and encourage you to think about the actions you take that demonstrate the behaviors.

Behavior	My Specific Actions
Being sincere and honest	• Followed workplace rules. • Asked for help when I needed it.
Perceived as authentic	• Did what I said I would do. • Accepted feedback and input with grace. • Looked others in the eye when speaking with them.

One of the behaviors in Chapter 1 that conveys authenticity is "being sincere and honest." I demonstrated being sincere and honest by following workplace rules and asking for help when it was needed. I know this is very basic, but when you're new in your career or even at a new job, it's scary to ask for help because you don't want people to think you don't know what you're doing. It's always good to ask for help when you need it rather than wasting time trying to figure out what to do or making unnecessary mistakes.

Some ways to be perceived as authentic include doing what you say you'll do, accepting feedback and looking people in the eye when you're speaking with them.

I once worked with a young woman named Rhonda. She was a college student who was interning in our department while attending a local university. In her interview, she seemed excited about working with us, expressed enthusiasm for learning Human Resources, talked about her desire to learn, and had a friendly way of expressing herself.

Once she started working with us, we could see that she was exactly who she portrayed herself to be and it was so refreshing. Sometimes people will say anything to get a job, but that doesn't serve anyone well. If you get the job, but lied about your interest or credentials, you'll eventually realize that the job isn't the one you want, or the company will realize that they shouldn't have hired you. Present yourself honestly in interviews.

After completing her internship with us, we hired Rhonda full-time and that was a great decision. Why? She is someone who works hard to learn everything possible and the quality of her work is very good. Her secret to success so far is that she knows she has much to learn, but she's anxious to build her skills and do work that she's capable of doing.

When Rhonda makes mistakes, she doesn't blame others; she admits that she made them, learns from the experience, and goes on about her work. In this early part of her career she is already a great example to other young professionals because she is showing them how to behave appropriately when the inevitable mistake happens.

Rhonda also has the confidence to laugh at herself when she's missed the mark on something because she knows that no one expects her to be perfect. She wasn't blowing off the mistakes; it was obvious that she cared that she made them and wanted to make it right. She just didn't beat herself up unnecessarily. She's gained the support of the senior members of the team and others in the organization. We all want her to succeed and I have no doubt that she will.

Unlike Rhonda, when I was just starting out in my career, I was terrified of making mistakes because I had no experience in the business world and couldn't predict how I would be treated if I made a mistake.

Before we look more closely at Rhonda's authentic behavior, in what ways can you relate to Rhonda? Do you take feedback in such a way that you learn from it, but you don't let it destroy your confidence? Do you present your credentials honestly in interviews? Do you do what you say you'll do when you say you'll do it?

Let's refer to the list of behaviors that convey authenticity in Chapter 1 again along with the specific ways that Rhonda demonstrates the behaviors:

Behavior	What She Did
Being sincere and honest	• Described herself honestly in interviews. • Admitted to her mistakes and learned from them.
Being yourself	• Contributed to work efforts and discussions. • Dressed in a way that fits company policies but also reflects her individual style.
Acting extroverted	• Tried to get to know others. • Volunteered at company events.
Perceived as authentic	• Did what she said she'd do. • Consistently did her best work. • Accepted and learned from feedback.
Standing up for your beliefs	• Contributed to employee resource councils.

There are countless ways that one can demonstrate authenticity. While I can't provide an all-inclusive list to you, I hope that these examples help you understand the general principles. For example, Rhonda could also demonstrate standing up for her beliefs by not gossiping at work because she believes that gossip is hurtful.

Now let's look at how Leo demonstrates authenticity. Leo is a very bright young man. His manager was thrilled when he accepted a junior position in her department. In addition to his normal work activities, he volunteered at various company events. I was impressed by his engaging personality, energy, and desire to help the organization right from the start.

The first time I met Leo at a company event he asked if he could meet with me. I was happy to meet with him because I made it a point to meet with as many employees as possible.

When Leo arrived at my office, it was as if an entirely different person showed up to see me. He looked angry, avoided even a mildly friendly greeting, and immediately began to share what felt like a list of grievances.

The first thing he said was that the office decor was "drab" and suggested that we repaint the walls in a more vibrant color. Next, he asked if I "ever" benchmarked some of our benefit plans because he felt our 401k was not as competitive as it should be. At this point I was getting irritated because he seemed to have made some broad and inaccurate assumptions.

Nonetheless, I explained to Leo that it wasn't likely that we would undertake such an expensive project as repainting the walls, but that every employee had the ability to decorate their workspace in a way that made them feel comfortable. I explained to him the extensive benchmarking that we did on an annual basis and our findings.

Lastly, he casually referred to his last performance appraisal as "a joke," saying that he didn't get anything from it at all because his manager wasn't effective. Ok, now I understood that he was there to let me know that his manager was, in his view, ineffective.

After our conversation, I thought about the two Leo's I'd seen in the short time he'd been at the organization. I read his performance appraisal to see what feedback he was given.

Contrary to the description Leo described to me, his manager had given him detailed and valuable feedback, but he wasn't willing to accept it from her. She highlighted his strengths and described specific aspects of his work that he could improve. She also mentioned that he needed to consider his audience when communicating with them. After seeing how Leo communicated with me, I knew she was spot on with her feedback. This should have been, but wasn't, a lightbulb moment for Leo!

I called Leo to share what I had read and that I thought it was clear, specific, and thoughtful. I asked him why he thought it was a joke and he responded with a snarl and said, "None of that stuff that she said I need to improve is true—she just doesn't like me."

Using the behaviors that convey authenticity from Chapter 1 as a guide, let's look at Leo's behavior and actions:

Behavior	What He Did
Acting extroverted	• Tried to get to know others. • Volunteered at company events.
Perceived as authentic	• Discounted rather than accepted feedback
Standing up for your beliefs	• Got involved in business resource councils.
Feeling that you're authentic	• Made negative assumptions about others' intentions.

I saw two different Leos in a short amount of time, so it was not possible to perceive him as being authentic. Leo #1 was engaged, thoughtful and seemed to care about the organization. Leo #2 was overly negative and unwilling to accept feedback. After my discussion with him that day in my office, I believed that hiring him may have been a mistake.

After Leo initially discounted his manager's feedback, I don't think he expected that I would take the time to read his review. I pointed out that his manager had given him specific examples of where he could improve and expressed her commitment to helping him. His manager handled his feedback perfectly. Leo was unwilling to consider the possibility that there was something he could learn from feedback. His natural tendency was to take the position that "it's not me, it's you!"

Know Thyself

> The Law of Awareness says you must know yourself to grow yourself.[25]

Leo isn't a self-aware person and apparently he's not alone. As researcher and psychologist Tasha Eurich learned in a four-year study about self-awareness, there are two types of people:

- Those who think they're self-aware (95% of all people).
- Those who are (10–15% of all people).

Eurich conducted significant research to understand how to have more self-awareness and shared some insights of her research in a TEDx talk. She shared that her team found so few genuinely self-aware people that they referred to them as "self-awareness unicorns."[26]

She goes on to say that "on a good day, 80 percent of us are lying to ourselves about lying to ourselves." Her study showed that people who were introspective were more stressed and less satisfied with their jobs and relationships and that the negative consequences increased the more they introspected. My reaction to her commentary was "so are we supposed to avoid introspection?"

Eurich explained that the problem with introspection is that most people ask *why* when they're being introspective, but they should be asking *what*. For example, Leo may have asked himself why he wasn't viewed as highly as he felt he deserved and concluded that his boss didn't like him. Had he been open to his manager's feedback and asked *what* he could do to improve, he might have learned something about how he was viewed at work and used that self-awareness to get what he wanted which I presume was a great career at our organization. His manager and I wanted that for him as well.

I had an aha moment about my early career behavior when I read Eurich's perspective. Because I started out at work with no education, no experience, and much humility, I often felt that if something wasn't going well, it had to be my fault, not someone else's. That wasn't always true of course, but that attitude influenced me to consider that there was some truth to feedback, and I should pay attention.

I worked hard to excel at work, and it was hard to hear that there were things I could do better. No one likes to hear that they fell short of expectations. Unlike Leo, I used to read my performance reviews repeatedly, analyzing every word. I was a performance review geek. I'd highlight my boss's commentary on anything that I didn't understand so I could ask about it.

I created goals based on their feedback and reminded myself what they wanted me to do differently.

Throughout my entire career, my managers' feedback meant so much to me that I would replay their words repeatedly in the wee hours of the night. I wanted to understand how I could improve and be the best performer possible.

Sometimes I also wanted to know why the guy in my department was making so much more than I was when he wasn't doing the work he was being paid to do. It is a fair question when in that situation. Sometimes I found the answer acceptable and sometimes I didn't, but my manager knew what was on my mind. We'll talk more about tough conversations later in this book.

Why Being Authentic at Work Matters

> *Find a group of people who challenge you, spend a lot of time with them, and it will change your life.*[27]
>
> —*Amy Poehler*

Work is both more productive and more fun when you have meaningful connections with your colleagues. Brené Brown defines connection as "the energy that is created between people when they feel seen, heard and valued—when they can give and receive without judgement."[28]

I can vividly recall once having a conversation with a young woman who used Brown's exact words with me when she asked for my help with her manager. She wanted to be seen, heard, and valued. She told me that whenever she spoke with her manager about taking on certain responsibilities, he would convert her story to *his* life experience. The problem with that is that his experiences were completely different than hers. He'd use his experience as the rationale for why she shouldn't want to do what she was describing. She was in a tough situation.

I advised her to tell her manager that their work experience and their goals were different. I suggested that she say, "I would appreciate it if you would see my request from my perspective rather than yours." Saying something like this helps the manager realize that he needs to listen.

In this case the manager genuinely wanted to help her, but he couldn't do that unless he could see things from her perspective rather than his. He was thinking that if the steps he took worked for him, they'd work for her. I intervened and explained this to him. He was genuinely unaware that by acting this way he was making her feel insignificant.

Being authentic at work matters for the success of a team as well. Twice in my career I have been on highly productive teams. What made the experiences so fun was that we knew each other as human beings, respected each other, and were willing to be vulnerable with each other. There was never any doubt that we were trying to do the best work possible together.

Because we were connected at an authentic and human level, we didn't second-guess intentions or hold meetings after meetings—things that waste time and are counterproductive. We were a great team and it's the best example of why I think being authentic at work matters. I knew that if I didn't know the answer to something I could just say "I don't know, but I'll find out" and not worry that they would think I was stupid.

Or if someone was struggling with something, I wanted to do everything possible to help.

If you find yourself on a highly effective team, know that it's a blessing. Learn all you can from this experience and take your learning with you to other teams when it's appropriate to do so.

New York executive coach Ora Shtull says, "When employees show up as wholly human at work, they create a ripple effect. Their willingness to live authentically gives those around them permission. This creates a work environment where talent is engaged and creative."[29]

Stephen Joseph says that authentic people cope better with stress, live more harmoniously with others, and have deeper relationships.[30] Think of the more meaningful relationships you have with people at work and in your personal life. Isn't it true that the deeper connections are with those who seem sincere and honest and comfortable in their own skin?

While the COVID-19 pandemic has been devastating on many fronts, one positive is that we've been given an opportunity to see our colleagues from a more human perspective. Out of necessity, some of the facades have come down. We're seeing cats walking across desks, children inadvertently coming into the room, and even sharing a good laugh about the likelihood that the person we're talking to probably has on pajama bottoms. And guess what? Most people don't care about the informality of the meetings, and that's a refreshing change.

I am optimistic that employers will start to believe that employees can be productive at home. Gallup's research indicates that "those who spend 60% to 80% of their time working remotely are the most likely to be engaged. And the less time they spend in the office, the more progress they make."[31]

Thankfully, most of us have now had an opportunity to learn more about ourselves and each other. I believe that this will be one of the great learnings about work from this crisis.

Does "being authentic" at work mean saying or acting on every thought, personality trait, or boundary that comes into your head, consequences be damned? Of course not.

Authenticity vs. Transparency

Authenticity means that your words and actions represent who you are and what matters to you. Transparency is the extent to which you share information.

For example, let's say that Jane is someone who cares about fitness. She stays active, eats healthy, and is always learning more about the benefits of a healthy diet. She decided to be a health coach because she wanted to help as many people as possible. She's a living, breathing example of her passion for fitness. This is being authentic.

The reason Jane cares so much is that her mother died of a massive heart attack at age forty-five. When she meets clients, she decides if she's going to share her mother's story based on her assessment of whether the story will help or hurt each individual client.

I think the word transparent is overused in organizations and seems to be used interchangeably with honesty. They're not the same. When companies say they're transparent with employees, they mean they're going to tell the truth and, of course, they should do so. But it's not likely that they're going to disclose exactly how they reached certain decisions.

I used to say, "I'm going to be fully transparent here." What I meant was that I had weighed several options. I'd describe those and say where I ran into challenges with one decision versus another. Sometimes I would share that I wasn't sure about a decision because I wasn't sure I had the best data set and as a result perhaps I was missing something. That's transparency.

So then, can you be authentic without being transparent? Absolutely, and Jane's story above is representative of that. Can you be transparent without being authentic? Yes. Social media is filled with people who are heart-stoppingly transparent about their daily lives and then later we learn that all was not what it seemed.

Authenticity Doesn't Mean Nice or Weak

> My attitude is that if you push me towards something that you think is a weakness, then I will turn that perceived weakness into a strength.[32]
>
> —Michael Jordan

One of the most authentic people I've ever worked with isn't someone who would be described as "nice" although he is highly professional. He is an expert in his field who is laser-focused on solving his clients' problems. As a result, he doesn't spend much time on small talk. He also won't tell someone that something is good if it's his opinion that it isn't.

As you build your career, seek people who are authentic in this way because they will be much more helpful to you than someone who tells you only what you want to hear. You may not like hearing what they have to say, but you can learn so much from them.

When I was just starting out in HR, there was a guy named Tony who headed up HR at one of our plants in another state. I worked hard to develop an employee communication piece and previewed it with him because I had heard that Tony was someone who knew the employees well. After reading what I had put together, he said something along the lines of "that kind of writing might work fine at "corporate" (sarcasm duly noted!), but if you send something like that to our plant guys, you're really going to piss 'em off." He was so right!

I learned an important lesson that day. I was so used to being a "corporate" person where communications are less personal that I failed to realize the needs of the people in the plants were different. I needed to better understand the people I was now serving. This is a lesson I've taken with me every step of the way.

I changed the communication so that it was more down to earth, and it got the message across in a way that was helpful to the employees. If Tony had simply said that the communication was "fine," my butt would have been handed to me and rightfully so. Without Tony's help, I might have lost credibility that would've taken years to get back.

Tony and I developed a great working relationship because we saw that together we could do better work than we could individually. I trusted him completely and appreciated his straightforward style.

No matter what position you hold, you can be like Tony. If you're in a situation where you see something at work that isn't right or good enough, speak up. Know that it's ok if your suggestion isn't accepted. Confident, thoughtful leaders will appreciate that you want to contribute to the organization.

Authenticity Doesn't Need Disclaimers

Sometimes weak people will use authenticity as an excuse for treating people badly or to mask their poor communication skills. When someone uses a disclaimer such as "I'm a straight shooter," "I always tell it like it is," or "I'm going to cut right to the chase because that's how I am," know that this person is actually saying, "Deep down, I know I don't have the skills to say this more effectively." A person like that is, in my opinion, often the most vocal because they lack confidence. I've run into a few of them in my career and thinking about their behavior still irritates me.

My point here is not that you should avoid difficult conversations or sugarcoat your commentary. Think about what you're going to say and say it without disclaimers. If you're truly a straight shooter, it'll be obvious, no disclaimer needed.

I have never met someone who is authentic yet weak. As you will learn in this book, being authentic takes guts. Spending the time necessary to know yourself is hard work and you're never done learning. To do that and to show up at work as authentically as possible is extraordinary and brave.

There Are Risks to Being Authentic

You might be thinking that being authentic at work is risky. You're right. Here are some risks that immediately come to mind:

- **Some people may not believe that you're being authentic and will be suspicious of your motives.** If you sense that this is the case and you care that they feel this way, invite the person to have coffee with you and ask if they have a concern that you can address. If you don't care that they feel this way, do nothing. How they feel isn't your problem to solve.

- **People will watch to see if your actions match your words.** You can't control what people think, but you can control what you do. Do what you say you will do.

- **You'll be vulnerable to criticism by others.** They may say you're too nice, too abrasive, too weak, and so on, and use this as an excuse for not supporting you. There are always going to be naysayers. If you chase after every one of them, you'll never get anything done. These kinds of people usually talk about others no matter what. If it matters to you that someone is criticizing you, ask them to explain why they're doing so. My experience is that people like this usually don't have the courage to explain their criticisms.

- **You may overshare and inadvertently make someone uncomfortable.** Sharing personal aspects of your life should be done with caution. If you feel you've over-shared, apologize. You can say something like "I am so sorry that I made you feel uncomfortable with my comments; that wasn't my intention."

- **You may share something about yourself and someone may use it against you when it's convenient to do so.** Sometimes it could be a fairly benign comment such as, "I feel so grateful to be doing the work I'm doing," that somehow gets conveyed to others as, "She's really happy doing what she does and isn't looking to be promoted." If you're aware that this occurred, you can address it by saying, "Yes, I do love what I do, but I'm always anxious to contribute at a higher level." Unfortunately, if the person is in a senior position and is deciding on a promotion, you may never know how your comment was misrepresented.

- **It's possible to become judgmental when someone else's authentic behavior isn't aligned with yours.** As you learn more about your authenticity, you will appreciate it in others and likely become less judgmental. Remember, we're all on our own unique journeys.

- **It's possible that, as you grow in your authenticity, you will experience shame about how you've behaved in the past.** Maybe you genuinely value kindness and compassion. When you think about your past, you may feel that you weren't kind to others. Or maybe you saw someone being mistreated and didn't say anything. Some of these feelings may come to the surface and cause you pain. It's never too late to apologize if you've unintentionally hurt someone. Do not carry shame with you into the future; it's a heavy load.

- **You might feel conflicted at work.** There will be times when your personal values and your company's policies may be at odds, so you'll need to decide the best action to take and accept the consequences. I've experienced this only a few times, primarily because I worked at companies that had values that aligned with my own.

One story that comes to mind happened years ago, when a group of HR people was working to purchase some new technology. The person in charge of procurement told us not to look the salespeople in the eye or express any friendliness toward them whatsoever. I thought that was the most ridiculous advice I'd ever heard, and I greeted them and thanked them for their time.

As you grow in your authenticity and career, there will be circumstances that you will find unacceptable. Consider what those might be and plan how you'll react if those circumstances occur.

Risks for People of Color and LGBTQIA

According to one survey, in the LGBTQIA community, "About 19% of respondents who are not out at work worry their careers would be ruined if they were, 70% are concerned coming out would make their colleagues uncomfortable around them."[33]

People of color face numerous risks as well. In a study of more than 300 African American, Hispanic, and other racial minority applicants to an MBA program indicated they'd be "more uncomfortable opening up to a white coworker than to a black one, especially if their work performance was average (as opposed to high)." They worried that "information highlighting their race (termed status-confirming disclosure) might reinforce the stereotypes that can undermine performance reviews and prevent progress toward leadership roles."[34]

There is still much work to do to make American workplaces diverse and inclusive. It's endlessly disappointing that we are not where we need to be.

I have seen firsthand and been inspired by the contributions made by those who participate in employee resource councils with the goal of furthering diversity and inclusion. The world is a diverse place, so business must be diverse as well. Employees can do their part, but leaders must stop talking about it and start making meaningful changes in their organizations.

In one article, Mick Mooney shared the following quote from Rajendra Agrawal, former general manager of the State Bank of India: "Living authentically is about living courageously; to live that way, you have to accept a level of risk as part of the process. If there was nothing risky about it, it wouldn't be considered courageous."[35]

What's in It for You to Be Authentic?

Life is short, and it's heartbreaking to see people spending it as someone they're not. We've discussed that being authentic isn't about disclosing everything about yourself, but rather discovering repeatedly who you truly are and bringing as much of your true self to work as you wish.

Research shows that those who believe they're authentic are more satisfied with their decisions, have a more positive sense of well-being, are motivated to pursue their goals, have more positive social relationships, and feel they're living the good life.[36]

Trying to be someone you're not takes a lot of energy that could be used in a more productive way. If you consistently feel that you're not being heard, that your thoughts don't seem to be important, or that you're completely disassociating with who you really are, then please stop and ask yourself if this is how you want to spend your precious life.

Amy Bucher summarizes what's in it for you so well:

> Being authentic brings happiness because it creates a setting where we indulge in the people and activities we love and avoid the ones we don't. When we are in situations that we may not have chosen, perhaps in the workplace, authenticity gives us permission to react in ways that feel honest and comfortable (within whatever strictures the situation puts forth).[37]

Amen to that! We are experiencing a time in our history where we must decide who we are and what we believe. Each of us was put on this planet for a reason. You were put on the planet for a reason, and it wasn't to be someone you're not. That's why authenticity matters. That's why YOU matter.

Key Takeaways

- Authenticity is about knowing yourself and defining what it means for you.
- Certain behaviors enable you to be perceived as authentic:
    - Being sincere and honest
    - Being yourself
    - Acting extroverted
    - Being perceived as authentic
    - Standing up for your beliefs
    - Feeling authentic
- People who are authentic at work cope better with stress and have deeper relationships with others.
- Being authentic comes with risks and benefits.

4 ARE YOU AUTHENTIC AT WORK?

I'm in the process of re-reading *Open Book*, Jessica Simpson's best seller, and have listened to the audio version at least twice. I wondered why I found her story so interesting and I finally understand why: her book shares the joys and sorrows of her journey to find and accept her authentic self.

I found the audio version incredibly powerful. Simpson's emotions are raw and powerful. She chokes back tears as she revisits painful memories such as being sexually abused by a family friend as well as enduring years of body-shaming. All of that was horrible enough, but she also had to grapple publicly with her failing marriage.

Can you imagine what all that must've been like for her? As I listened to her story, I better understood her as a person, not as a celebrity. She felt from a young age that she could change the world with her voice – this was her purpose. She lost her way more than once, but has reawakened her authenticity and is now sharing her story to help others.

I used to watch her reality show, *Newlyweds: Nick and Jessica,* which debuted in 2003. Before we were keeping up with the Kardashians, we were keeping up with Simpson and her then-husband Nick Lachey. The show positioned Simpson as the beautiful, not-so-bright, singing damsel in distress and Lachey as the serious, sullen knight who would come to her rescue.

Simpson was portrayed as someone incapable of doing much for herself, including basic things like laundry or cooking. She was young, and it made for interesting TV for her to be "helpless." By her own admission, her life became something she acted as a way of completing the requisite episodes.

By season two, it was obvious that we were watching a marriage disintegrate on TV. And then the girl who seemingly couldn't make a decision made a powerful one: she pulled the plug on the marriage. By her account, when she told her mother she was filing for divorce, her mother encouraged her to hang in there and said, "You are America's couple." Simpson responded, "What is the point in being a power couple if we're faking it? There's no real power in this anymore. Real power is in authenticity." So true!

It wasn't easy, but she found her power. She launched a billion-dollar fashion empire, wrote her book, continued her music career, and focused on overcoming an alcohol addiction so she could grow her brand, be a good wife, mother, and more. While she has money and fame, her life has been filled with public victories, painful relationships, setbacks, humiliation, and, like all of us, fear. She said the following:

"I've come to recognize fear when I see it. It may show itself in different ways, but it's a familiar face, isn't it? I have a different relationship with fear now. I've learned that we grow from walking through it and a lot of people don't even know they have that option. You either conquer it or you let it destroy you."[38]

When I think about the Simpson we saw on the show and the powerhouse who has publicly shared her story, the difference is startling. She's evolved from being highly dependent on others to someone who's learned to trust her own instincts and accept the resulting successes and failures.

While most of us aren't celebrities, our life stories are no less important. Our legacy is the ultimate reflection of how we've spent our lives.

In some ways creating a legacy can be compared to painting a picture. Our legacy is the completed painting while the brush strokes are the decisions we make along the way. Sometimes our painting doesn't unfold the way we imagined and that's ok. I can tell you that often our imaginations fall far short of what we're capable of creating. Will we make mistakes? Of course! Most of the time, we can correct them and continue painting the picture.

It's important to be deliberate about what we're trying to create in our lives. Using our art analogy, if we were setting out to paint a floral painting, we would build a concept in our mind of what we want the painting to look like, select the appropriate colors, the properly sized canvas and we'd go about painting our work of art.

In my mind, there's no more important work of art than your legacy. Like works of art, each of us is a one-of-a-kind, authentic masterpiece created to live our purpose. Is the way you're spending your life reflective of what means most to you?

It's OK if you haven't thought much about your legacy; most of us don't until we are middle-aged, and we start feeling that our time on the planet is passing more quickly than we'd like. When I was younger, I thought that legacies were reserved for old, wealthy people. I was so busy working, caring for my family, and going to school that legacy-building never entered my mind. But I was building a legacy, nonetheless. So are you. Stop and think about that for a moment: you're building *your* legacy.

I'm going to share a story about someone who's built a tremendous legacy, but I want you to know that a legacy is deeply personal. If you're a great friend who's always been there for others, that's a tremendous legacy. Great parent? Amazing legacy. Great colleague? Yep, amazing legacy.

Brian Floriani comes to mind when I think of legacy building. In a TEDx Talk, he shared the profound impact the same day deaths of his grandmother and father had on his life and career. Floriani had been living the good life and was the epitome of success. He was the lead instructor with the Golf Digest Schools, living in Lake Tahoe in the summer and West Palm Beach in the winter. As he delivered eulogies for two of the most important people in his life, he reflected on what his own eulogy might be. In particular, he wondered if upon his death (a) would anyone have anything to say about him, (b) would it be true, and (c) would it matter. His answers were "not really," "probably not," and "no." He realized that despite his lucrative career, he wasn't fulfilled and felt extremely empty. He realized, "Though I was successful, I was far from significant." [39]

As he shifted his thinking from success to significance, Floriani thought about becoming an elementary school teacher, but became a reading paraprofessional as a way in the door. That experience changed his life because he saw first-hand the profound impact that reading proficiency can have on someone's life. He went on to found Bernie's Book Bank, a wonderful organization named for his father that collects and distributes books to children in need. At the time of this writing, 18,247,811 books have been given away. He found what significance means for him.

I've had the pleasure of meeting Floriani a few times. I love the look on someone's face when they're doing what they're meant to do. He has that look.

Both Simpson and Floriani felt empty despite being incredibly successful in their work. They followed their hearts to authenticity and their lives and work are now more fulfilling. This kind of transformation doesn't happen unless there's a genuine desire for change.

Now back to you. You will spend roughly a third of your life at work before you retire. Are you able to bring your authentic self to work? Do you feel connected to the work you're doing? Are you living a life of significance? If the answers to these questions are "yes," take a moment to express your gratitude to the universe. I'm serious—this is a blessing! If not, read on.

Signs That You're Not Feeling Connected to Your Work

If you're not feeling connected to your work, you're either not doing the work that matters most to you and/or you're not bringing your authentic self to work to the extent you'd like. Do any of these signs apply to you?

You Dread Going to Work

Despite its name, I've always liked Jeff Foxworthy's "You might be a redneck if…." comedy routine, so I'll use it with a twist here. You might dread going to work if you do the following:

- Toss and turn most nights
- Spend your free time with friends complaining about how much you dread going to work
- Call off sick more than you should, even when you're not sick
- Fantasize about quitting your job the first chance you get
- Don't have meaningful relationships with the people you work with
- Can't think of anything you're excited about at work

All the above are symptoms, but it's easy to know if you dread going to work, isn't it? I've dreaded going to work only twice in forty years, but both situations were excruciatingly difficult. No matter how hard I tried (and let me tell you, I tried), I couldn't convince myself that staying in those situations was worth the heartache I was feeling. And you know what? I don't think anyone should stay in a situation that's not fulfilling. At some point when you know that things won't get better, why stay?

When I reflect on the times I dreaded going to work, I didn't want to accept that I was unhappy because I was ashamed to do so. I was ashamed that I could be unhappy when I had so many blessings. I was paid well, did amazing work, and genuinely cared about my colleagues.

While I was able to find gratitude every day, I couldn't find joy and joy matters greatly to me. It took me many years to realize that I deserved to be joyful at work. Once I knew how important this was to me, I wasn't going to work without joy again. I do my best work when I am filled with joy and gratitude. So do you.

When we dread going to work, we feel it don't we? It starts from the moment you wake up. Instead of feeling happy about going to work, you wish you had something better to do. As you sit at your desk, you may sigh and think to yourself "here we go again." Everything seems to require more mental and physical energy than it should. You feel tired before you even begin the day.

If you are feeling this way, but haven't really thought about why, look at the list below and ask yourself if any of them are the reasons you dread going to work. Take note of those that apply to your situation and write down any other reasons that come to mind that aren't in the list below:

- You have a strained relationship with your boss.
- You don't trust your boss.
- You don't like or get along with your coworkers.
- You feel taken advantage of.
- You struggle with balancing life and work.
- You feel underutilized.
- You have too much work to do and are overwhelmed.
- You've done something wrong and are worried you'll get caught.

- You've seen someone else do something wrong and don't know what you should do about it.
- Your values and those of your company are not aligned.
- Someone has asked you to do something that you're not willing to do.
- It's a bunch of things and you're just "done"—you want out.

What did you discover by considering the possible reasons for dreading going to work? Were you aware that this is how you felt? Did you know the reasons for your dread but didn't want to acknowledge them?

Keep your notes and think about how you're feeling. We will discuss how to share your thoughts with others later in this chapter and throughout the book.

You Feel Like an Imposter

> *The biggest insecurity I had was my singing. Even though I had sold 70 million records, there was this feeling like, I'm not good at this.*[40]
>
> *— Jennifer Lopez*

If Jennifer Lopez feels like an imposter, it's understandable that it can happen to anyone.

Kristen Weir describes the imposter phenomenon as feelings that usually occur among "high achievers who are unable to internalize and accept their success. They often attribute their accomplishments to luck rather than to ability, and fear that others will eventually unmask them as a fraud." She goes on to say that people who feel like imposters often grew up in families where there was so much pressure to achieve that one's self-worth is determined by achieving. This is also a common feeling among minorities. Here's what she says about this:

> That's not terribly surprising to Frederick Hives, a fourth-year PsyD candidate at John F. Kennedy University. Hives struggled with impostor feelings throughout grad school and says he often feels like he's progressed not on his own merits, but due to sympathy from others. As an African American student, Hives says, "I was taught I would need to work twice as hard to be half as good. While this instills a goal-oriented approach within me, it also keeps me feeling as though my efforts will never be enough."[41]

I used to have a young man on my team named David who was exceptionally talented. I thought his work was spectacular and told him so on a regular basis. He and I talked at length about his challenging childhood and how hard he worked to have a different life than he had growing up. I saw tremendous potential in him and genuinely appreciated him as a team member and young professional.

Unfortunately, David seemed to struggle with imposter syndrome. He would ask me a question and I would answer him, almost always agreeing completely with his thoughtful proposals. I'd leave the conversation feeling good about it but would later learn that he was convinced that I was thinking something judgmental or negative about him. This was a head-shaker to me because he seemed to go out of his way to diminish how people felt about his contributions.

I started to see a pattern where he'd seem to create these stories in his mind, and they became so troubling to him that he felt that his only choice was to leave the organization. I was completely baffled but concluded that he needed more from his manager than I could give him.

He subsequently left several other employers because he felt his managers didn't understand or appreciate him as well. I suspect that they saw in him what I saw: an incredibly talented guy who could never receive enough recognition to offset his perhaps unconscious feeling that he didn't deserve the success that he had rightfully earned.

It's not unusual to feel like an imposter at some point in your career. If you feel this way, it's good to have this awareness and to explore what's behind your feelings. If you're new in your career, give yourself time to excel; your feelings may simply be due to lack of experience. If you're not new to your career, something more serious may be contributing to your feelings. Talk to people you trust and ask for their insights and read articles on this topic.

You Don't Share Your Ideas

Do you find that you don't share your ideas because you feel they'll be ignored or diminished in some way? You have contributions to make, but why bother? It's difficult to be authentic if you aren't "being" at work, right?

Once I was on a team where the department head held weekly meetings. I had recently joined the organization and was excited to work with the team because they were smart and had great ideas. I noticed a strange dynamic at the meetings in that only a few people talked and everyone else seemed checked out. They'd look at their phones, draw pictures or daydream—perhaps about getting out of those meetings. What seemed even more interesting was that the few who talked either didn't notice or didn't care that no one else was included in the conversation. Three people would talk and about ten wouldn't. It was so weird!

After a few of these "meetings," I asked some of them why they didn't say anything. They said that it was clear to them that their thoughts didn't matter. That was a logical explanation because that's how they were being treated.

I felt strongly that if I was going to stay there, I was going to contribute. I started sharing ideas and comments at the meeting and the others started pitching in as well. We decided that if we had to sit there every week, we were going to say something. The meetings were a little better going forward, but admittedly things were still weird because the leader wasn't really equipped to lead a large team well.

Bruce Katcher, president of Discovery Surveys, found that "half of all employees are too scared to openly express their views at work."[42] If this statistic is true, no wonder businesses struggle with managing change, managing risk, and retaining talent.

Jay Steinfeld provides some good insights into why people don't speak up:[43]

- Fear of retaliation or looking stupid
- The appearance of challenging authority

- Previous bad experiences
- Lack of skill with practical candor (an employee unfamiliar with the practice of giving feedback in a trustworthy but honest manner may feel that their comments are rude or unwelcome).
- The manager's door isn't really "always open."

I was on another team where the leader surrounded herself with what I can only describe as a clique, the kind that you might see in high school. The group had worked for her for years and were understandably comfortable with each other, yet there was a strange dynamic between them that I never understood.

She would criticize individuals in front of the full team, usually raising her voice and commenting on something she felt they missed or could've done better. Whenever she realized she misunderstood something (this was often the case) and overreacted, she rarely apologized for her excessively harsh criticisms. Some of those who were humiliated looked so hurt while others looked ambivalent. Work shouldn't be this way. I decided that I wouldn't allow her to treat me this way and I went about planning how I'd respond given certain situations.

The people on her team were seasoned pros yet they consistently sat quietly and took her wrath. I learned to expect that someone would be the target of a smackdown at most meetings. The more I witnessed it, the more troubling I found it to be because that's not how people should be treated. People shouldn't ever have to condition themselves to be humiliated.

When people fear their leader, they do exactly what her team members did: they share what they feel will help them avoid the most wrath and they work in fear. I don't know why those seasoned pros found that behavior acceptable, but they did. I didn't.

If you find yourself in a situation like this, the most effective approach is to do your best work and prepare well. If the leader challenges the work or raises concerns, listen to their questions, and respond thoughtfully. Do your best to avoid being defensive (even if you feel defensive on the inside) and respond to their questions.

In the situation I described above, the team members should have said, "I think it's possible you've misunderstood some of the key points," and then indicate what those happen to be. Or say, "I am so glad you've asked about whether we took those steps; we agree those are important. This is what we discovered when we did that work (describe your findings)."

It's not fulfilling to work for someone who is volatile and inconsistent. If they're far along in their career, they're not going to change. You'll have to decide to accept this treatment or to leave. I hope you will know that you deserve better and leave if you're ever in this situation. But use this as an example of the kind of leader that you will not become. I used to have a manager who told me that sometimes the best examples are bad ones. Learn from it and be better.

When team members fear their leaders to the extent that they're not comfortable speaking up, it's not only a lousy experience, it's detrimental to the organization. This is not a path to authenticity and, if you're in this situation, I guarantee it's the result of bad leadership.

Sometimes bad leaders are removed from organizations and unfortunately sometimes they get promoted. You will have to decide what is acceptable to you in your work situation, but I hope you'll know that you deserve better and decide your next steps accordingly. Are you afraid to speak up? Are you afraid to leave? If so, why?

You Don't Speak Up About Things That Matter to You

> *In the end, we will remember not the words of our enemies, but the silence of our friends.*[44]
>
> —*Martin Luther King, Jr.*

There have been times in my life when I've heard people say racist or homophobic things in front of me and I was silent. I'm ashamed to share that with you. I was afraid to say something in some cases, while in others I didn't know what to say. With time and maturity, I gained confidence and now I have zero tolerance for discrimination of any kind.

Years ago, I was at a meeting where a guy in my department made a racist comment about Mexicans saying that they should "swim back to where they came from." I said nothing, but that comment was personal to me: my grandmother crossed the border illegally from Mexico to give birth to my father. Most people are aware enough at work to realize when they've said something so inappropriate, but he proceeded to make the comment again in a different meeting. I was very junior and didn't know what I should do, and unfortunately no one else spoke up.

I talked to my manager and he told me he'd speak to the guy, but he didn't. He probably thought that no one would be ignorant enough to say something like that again, but he was wrong. It took three times before his behavior was addressed.

One survey of over 3,000 employees showed that 40 percent hide their connection to an ethnic or religious group and 37 percent hide their support of issues such as civil unions or gender equality. Fifty-three percent of the survey respondents felt that their managers expected them to cover. "Sometimes, this came across when people stayed silent when confronted by other people's opposing beliefs; a gay-rights activist refrained from speaking up when a manager said homophobic things."[45]

Covering who you are has negative psychological consequences. It takes a toll on you when you cover who you are, and it drains you of energy that could be spent in a more healthy and productive way. It's bad for companies for the same reason. Companies spend significant amounts of money measuring employee engagement but speaking thoughtfully to employees and enabling them to do the same is key to building engagement.

It's hard to reconcile that more than half of managers expect people to cover while simultaneously touting their commitment to inclusion and diversity. It's difficult to accept that companies are committed to inclusion and diversity when most companies have few people of color in their C-suites and virtually none on their boards. No wonder people avoid speaking up about what matters to them.

Good leaders who are committed to inclusion and diversity enable authenticity. In his book *Covering: The Hidden Assault on Our Civil Rights*, Kenji Yoshino says, "My real commitment is to autonomy—giving individuals the freedom to elaborate their authentic selves, rather than to a rigid notion of what constitutes an authentic gay identify."[46]

Do you speak up about what matters to you? If not, why?

You Avoid Sharing Anything Personal About Yourself at Work

If you don't share anything personal about yourself at work, ask yourself why that is the case. As I've said earlier, I don't think it's appropriate or necessary to share everything about yourself. But if your colleagues know nothing about you personally, it might mean that you simply don't feel a connection with them. I think connections with your colleagues are important in doing your best work.

Do you share anything personal about yourself at work? If not, why?

Exercise

I've shared several examples that should help you complete this exercise. What are two to three areas where being more authentic would benefit you and your employer the most? What steps could you take to improve things? Make notes in the chart below. We'll talk more about communicating your thoughts in the following chapters.

Feelings	What Will Make It Better?
I dread going to work	
I feel like an imposter	
I don't share my ideas	
I don't speak up about things that matter to me	
I don't share anything personal about myself at work	
Other	

Face Your Fears

> Don't let the fear of striking out hold you back.[47]
> —Babe Ruth

Before we close out this chapter, we must talk about the F-word: fear. None of us like to admit that we're afraid to do or say things, but fear often gets in our way. Fear can also serve as an excuse for playing small or not taking charge of your life.

Sometimes, instead of admitting that we're afraid to work more authentically, we blame others for not doing so. The people we're blaming usually have no idea that we feel the way we do and have no intention of preventing us from being more authentic.

Jack Canfield, author of *The Success Principles*, one of my favorite leadership books describes fear this way:

- **F**antasized
- **E**xperiences
- **A**ppearing
- **R**eal

Canfield goes on to say, "Because we are the ones doing the fantasizing, we are also the ones who can stop fear and bring ourselves into a state of clarity and peace by facing the actual facts, rather than giving in to our imaginations."[48]

Mike Robbins also talks about fear in his book *Be Yourself, Everyone Else Is Already Taken*: "When it comes right down to it, the reason that many of us don't do or say what is true for us is that we're scared. We worry about failing, being rejected, disappointing others, being judged, and much more. We also worry, ironically, about succeeding."[49]

Let's look at some common fears at work. See if any of them ring true for you.

Fear of Getting Fired

Over the years I had several conversations with people who were really upset about something but didn't want to speak with their manager about it. They were convinced that if they shared their thoughts with their manager, they'd get fired. I've never seen someone get fired for this, ever.

It's easy to tell ourselves stories isn't it? We decide that it's best to not rock the boat or maybe we convince ourselves that no one really cares so why bother speaking up.

I understand why one would be afraid of losing a job, but my point here is that unless you're wildly unprofessional or incompetent, it's not likely you will lose your job for speaking with your manager about a concern.

Fear of Failing

> *Each of us must confront our own fears, must come face to face with them. How we handle our fears will determine where we go with the rest of our lives. To experience adventure or to be limited by the fear of it.*[50]
>
> — *Judy Blume*

Fear of failure prevents us from doing all kinds of things. I've been guilty of this more times than I can count. You work so hard to get from one place to another in life so why take a chance and blow it? And yet, when you know that you can do something and then chicken out, you get mad at yourself or you get mad at the person who wasn't afraid of going for it. Does this sound like you?

I have friends and acquaintances who do this all the time. There's a woman I know who is smart and capable, but she's worked for minimum wage her whole life. She has expressed interest in and could easily do administrative work making twice as much as she does now, but she makes no effort to get anything other than a minimum wage job. It's sad to watch, but indecision is a decision.

Sometimes just having someone tell you that they see your potential gives you the nudge you need to take a chance. I had an assistant who was incredibly intelligent (actually, all my assistants have been amazing). I told her she had the ability to do more if she wanted to do so and that I would help her. She was so excited! Before long she was doing amazing work in the benefits area and was feeling accomplished and happy while also providing outstanding support to employees.

Here's the deal: no one will know that you feel you can do more if you don't tell them. So, if this describes you, you've got to speak up. We'll talk more about how to do that later in the book, but one step you can take is to mention your aspirations to your manager in your performance discussion. Make sure you also include the same information in the document so that anyone looking at it will know that you've expressed an interest in doing more.

Fear of Succeeding

When my kids were small, I worried that if I were too successful, I wouldn't be there for them the way I wanted to be. I decided that I wasn't willing to disrupt my family for my job. Later in life, I was able to spend more time at work and that was fine. But when the kids were little, they were my priority and I'm proud of that decision.

I think that when a manager and an employee have a good relationship, there are honest conversations about what success looks like and what's possible within the context of one's life. I hope that you have this relationship with your manager; it makes all the difference in the world. I had good relationships with most of my managers (over twenty!) and I was able to have discussions like this with them.

Here's how Mike Robbins explains fearing success:

While fear of failure seems pretty straightforward, fear of success is a little more complex. Our reasons for being scared of success can vary from not enjoying the extra responsibility (for what it takes to create and maintain success and then what will people expect from us); not wanting to give up our struggle, stress, and negativity (even though we complain about these things, many of us secretly get off on the drama and self-pity at the same time); or worrying that people won't like us anymore (because we all love to make fun of and tear down people who succeed in our society).[51]

Fear of Rejection

No one wants to be rejected; it hurts, and we aren't usually well-equipped to deal with its impact. Have you not spoken up about something you want at work because you are afraid you'll be rejected? I've had managers tell me that they didn't think I could do something after I asked for a specific role or increased responsibility. When they said "no," it made my resolve even stronger. I look at those no's as gifts.

I remember once telling my manager that I wanted to be a tax analyst. I was only about twenty-two at the time and this was aspirational because I'd have to have a degree and some additional training. I was willing to do the work to get there. My manager at the time could've encouraged me while also acknowledging that it would take a long time to qualify for the role. Instead he literally laughed out loud and said it would never happen.

I never forgot the hurt that I felt. His behavior that day was something I kept in mind every time I thought that getting a degree wasn't possible. I told myself that one day I'd prove him wrong and I did. I never became a tax analyst, but that's because I was destined for other things. Don't let assholes ever diminish your dreams.

Let me say this to you. Your manager has been rejected before—I guarantee it. They may not admit it to you, but they've had the experience at least once. What's the worst thing that can happen if you ask for something and they say no? Years from now you won't regret that you asked and were rejected; you'll regret that you didn't ask. If you need help preparing for a discussion, talk to someone who can help and complete the exercises in this book.

Fear of Judgment

I grappled with this for years. And now that people can anonymously post anything they want about someone on social media and share it with thousands in an instant, there's a real reason to fear judgment. It happens all the time. Think of this as practice because the more you advance in an organization, the more you will be judged by others.

I personally think the best way to counteract judgement is to simply do your best at everything you do. No one can ask more of you than that, can they? Everyone makes mistakes, and if you make one, apologize, learn from it, and move on.

When my kids were growing up and dealing with others' perceived judgment, I would often tell them that people weren't thinking about them all that much and it's probably true for most of us. Let it go.

Fear of Messing Up What's "Fine"

Maybe you just want to play it safe because everything is fine. In his powerful book *Wake Up! Your Life Is Calling*, Mike Jaffe talks about the word "fine:"

> I say fine is a four-letter word. We get lured into fine's lair, giving us just enough success, just enough happiness, and just enough comfort to get sleepy. It makes us complacent, tricking us into believing that fine is where we need to remain. It starts planting its roots into us, making us attached to the way things are in our fine life. It deprives us of the urgency we once felt to create more for our lives! It skews our vision and thoughts into believing that we must define fine at all costs and that more than fine is dangerous, even selfish. We start to worry about what we're risking if we seek more, aim higher, and play bigger.[52]

Jaffe's book is outstanding. His story is indeed a wakeup call and I hope you'll consider reading his book.

Exercise

We've explored different types of fear. Did any of them ring true for you? This exercise is designed to help you name your fear by completing a very simple statement. As you're doing so, think about your fears including the people who contribute to your fear.

Ready? Complete this sentence:

I worry that if I _____, then [what

will happen?] _____.

I've included some sample statements in the following pages that may help you complete this exercise. If you have multiple fears, complete the sentence above for each one that applies.

My fear is that I'll get fired.

- I worry that if I see an injustice at work and speak up about it, then I'll lose my job.

My fear is failing.

- I worry that if I ask for a challenging assignment and fail, then my career is over.
- I worry that if I speak up for something that's important and it's not perceived well or doesn't deliver the results I thought it would, then I'll lose my credibility.

My fear is that I'll succeed.

- I worry that if I take on a challenging assignment and do it well, then the bar will just be made higher for me and I won't be able to succeed at the next level.
- I'm worried that if I succeed, then there will be demands placed on me that I won't be able to manage.
- I'm worried that if I share my expertise and it goes well with upper management, then my boss might feel threatened and I value our relationship.
- I worry that if I succeed, then I'm just setting myself up to fail at the next level.

My fear is rejection.

- I worry that if I share with my boss that I want to work elsewhere in the company, then they'll reject my request and I'll be forced to leave the company.
- I worry if I tell my manager that we aren't connecting in a way that's helpful to me, then they'll take it out on me, and I'll only have made things worse.

My fear is judgment.

- I worry that if I speak up at the next team meeting, then I'll be judged by others, especially if I don't say everything perfectly.
- I worry that if I share that I am gay, then people on my team will treat me differently than they do now.
- I worry that if I tell my boss that I need to work more reasonable hours because I want to spend time with my family, then they'll think I'm less dedicated and I'll never be promoted again.

Exercise

What resonated with you in this chapter? The first exercise in this chapter was designed to help you identify two or three feelings and actions that would improve them. In the second exercise you named your fear(s).

Now let's bring it all together. Here's an example to help you see how this exercise works:

Feelings	What Will Make It Better? (What Will I Do?)	What Am I Afraid of?	How Can I Overcome My Fear? (What Will I Do?)
I dread going to work because I have too much to do and I don't feel I'll ever catch up.	I need to give my boss some specific examples of why I feel this way and I need their help to make work more manageable.	I'm afraid they'll think I'm incompetent and will fire me.	I will provide specific examples of my workload and ask my boss to help me prioritize. I will provide suggestions for solving the problem. I will apply my boss's suggestions and prepare regular updates on how things are going.

Here's the grid for you to complete:

Feelings	What Will Make It Better? (What Will I Do?)	What Am I Afraid of?	How Can I Overcome My Fear? (What Will I Do?)

What do you now understand that you didn't before? Do your fears surprise you? There are two columns that specifically ask you to identify what you will do. When will you complete them? We will talk later in the book about how to create an action plan and commit to completing it.

Key Takeaways

- You might not be authentic at work if you do the following:
  - Dread going to work
  - Feel like an imposter
  - Don't share ideas
  - Don't speak up about things that matter to you
  - Don't share anything personal

- Fear can be nothing more than "fantasized experiences appearing real," but it can nonetheless play a significant role in hindering your authenticity. Understanding your fears is an important step in becoming more authentic.

- Completing the exercises in this chapter will help you identify what you're feeling, what you're afraid of and strategies for overcoming your fears.

5 AUTHENTICITY BASICS

We ended Chapter 4 with a grid to help you consider your feelings, fears, and ways to make things better. I'm bringing the grid forward and adding more details and examples that I hope will help you see how powerful it can be in building your authenticity.

If you were to get together with friends with the goal of defining beauty, how likely would it be that you'd all land on the same definition? The Mona Lisa is beautiful to some, but plain to others. Robert Redford is beautiful to me (*really* beautiful), but you might think he's old and wrinkled (no offense to him, of course).

Beauty is subjective, and guess what? So is authenticity. Earlier in the book I shared some general definitions posed by researchers. None of them are wrong, but what's right for you? Only you can define your authenticity. I want to help.

In Chapter 3 we looked at what it means to be authentic at work, along with the inherent risks and benefits of doing so. Did you see yourself or any of your authenticity challenges in any of the stories? Did you discover aspects of your life where you're less authentic than you'd like to be? Are there aspects of your life that would be more satisfying if you approached them more authentically? What's getting in the way?

Gentle reminder: You were put on earth for a reason and you have a limited amount of time to bring that reason to life. Can you live up to that reason without being yourself? Maya Angelou said the following:

> *Try to live your life in a way that you will not regret years of useless virtue and inertia and timidity. Take up the battle, take it up! It's yours, this is your life.*[53]

Angelou is an inspirational example to all that our past doesn't define our future. She was sexually abused and had an incredibly difficult life, but she persevered through it all and became a celebrated poet, civil rights activist and undeniably one of the most influential voices of our time. Her book *I Know Why The Caged Bird Sings* is powerful.

Chapter 4 provided reasons why you may not be taking your authentic self to work and the role that fear may be playing in that decision. Jen Sincero, author of *You Are a Badass,* posted on Facebook: "To fear or not to fear, that is the question." So true!

The exercises in Chapter 4 will help you understand your fears as well as ways that you can be more authentic.

Here's the grid we saw in Chapter 4. It's completed based on a real-life situation faced by my friend Paula:

Feelings	What Will Make It Better? (What Will I Do?)	What Am I Afraid of?	How Can I Overcome My Fear? (What Will I Do?)
I dread going to work because I have too much to do and I don't feel I'll ever catch up.	I need to give my boss some specific examples of why I feel this way and I need their help to make work more manageable.	I'm afraid they'll think I'm incompetent and will fire me.	I will provide specific examples of my workload and ask my boss to help me prioritize. I will provide suggestions for solving the problem. I will apply my boss' suggestions and prepare regular updates on how things are going.

Here are some additional details that will help you understand Paula's story. Paula has decades of experience, knows her stuff, and has been instrumental in countless successful efforts in her career. She takes great pride not only in the quality of her work, but also in the quantity she produces. Her work is deeply personal to her and she puts a lot of pressure on herself to deliver results, even when the demands placed on her are excessive and unreasonable.

Paula identifies so closely with her ability to deliver results that when she's unable to meet impossible demands, she blames herself. This causes a downward spiral where she worries that her reputation will be ruined and/or she'll be fired. She carries this worry with her every day.

Instead of asking for help or relief from the demands, she pushes herself even harder to achieve the impossible. As you can imagine, this makes her anxious, which causes her to lose sleep, barely eat, and sacrifice precious time with her family and friends.

Her authentic self is extroverted, fun-loving, caring, genuine, honest, thoughtful, deliberate, and effective. However, when she doesn't set boundaries, she allows people to take advantage of her and her authenticity is nowhere to be found. She works night and day out of fear of disappointing others or losing her job. She risks losing much more than her job; she risks losing *herself*.

The grid and the background information I shared capture the serious nature of Paula's current situation. While I've not mastered meditation yet, if I were Paula, I would spend time thinking about each column in the grid and consider how those feelings and fears are impacting the quality of my life. Reflecting in this way is difficult because it surfaces strong, sometimes painful emotions, but it is the only path to claiming a healthier situation.

Before we move on, I want to share one more grid and story with you. This time we're talking about Anna. Anna doesn't feel seen, appreciated, or supported. Her manager doesn't meet or engage with her regularly. In fact, she's shown little interest in Anna's area of expertise or in getting to know Anna as a person. Her manager is missing out because Anna is amazing.

I've known Anna for quite some time. She's incredibly talented and cares deeply about delivering high-quality work, and her expertise is in an area of utmost importance to most organizations. She's highly marketable, but she cares about the organization where she works and wants to see the work she's been doing through to completion.

Anna is hurt that she's been ignored and diminished. While she doesn't believe that her situation will dramatically improve, she has used the grid to develop some strategies for how she will conduct herself until she decides when or if she will leave the organization.

While Anna can't control her manager's feelings toward her, she can control the quality of her work and the ways that she will engage with her manager. She's noted those strategies in the grid. I was touched that Anna was so honest with herself and acknowledged that she is afraid of saying out loud that she doesn't feel valued. I know that it hurts to feel this way.

Here's Anna's grid:

Feelings	What Will Make It Better? (What Will I Do?)	What Am I Afraid of?	How Can I Overcome My Fear? (What Will I Do?)
I'm not valued for my contributions at work.	I need to have some-one in senior management understand what I do,	I'm afraid of saying out loud that I don't feel valued.	I will accept that some people will never value me or my contributions,

Feelings	What Will Make It Better? (What Will I Do?)	What Am I Afraid of?	How Can I Overcome My Fear? (What Will I Do?)
Despite consistently delivering strong results, my manager doesn't think I'm important enough to meet with regularly. I've hit a wall. It hurts that my manager hasn't even tried to know me. I need to find a different job. I'll take any job just to start over.	the contributions I've made, and help me gain the support I need in order to succeed.	If I say I'm not valued then I will be vulnerable and that will intensify my frustration, which will lead me to lose control of whether or when I leave.	but I won't let that get in the way of the pride I feel for my work. I will stop waiting for my manager to meet with me. I will request time and share my contributions, key outcomes, and what help I need. I'm going to work hard to find a job at a company that values the work I do and is committed to helping me succeed. I won't settle for less than I deserve.

Anna's grid is a bit of a manifesto. She's rightfully confident about herself and her work. Her strategy feels empowering to her and she's going to keep a printed version of it nearby so that she can continue to remind herself of how she's going to proceed.

I talked to Anna recently and she sounded like a new person. She said that she is determined to share her thoughts at work and contribute in the way that she is capable. She accepts that the relationship she has with her manager is not likely to change. She feels more in control of her future and I have no doubt that she's going to be wildly successful.

I hope that Paula and Anna's examples are helpful to you as you complete the grid for yourself.

Here are some authenticity basics that may be helpful to bringing more of yourself to work.

Say What You Mean and Mean What You Say

> *If you are patient in one moment of anger, you will escape one hundred days of sorrow.*[54]
>
> —*Chinese proverb*

Don't say things you don't mean because it's hard to take words back once they're said. Even after an apology, harsh words will never be forgotten. People who take great pride in saying *anything* they feel with little to no concern for how those words impact others usually aren't trusted.

I'm not suggesting that you shouldn't speak up, but rather that you think about what you're going to say and then say what you mean in a clear, concise manner.

In addition, avoid using disclaimers when you're speaking at work. For example, don't say, "I probably shouldn't say this," or "I know this is a dumb question." You are a professional and you don't need disclaimers.

Don't Lie

Just tell the truth. It's not always easy, but it's far better than having to explain why you lied once you're caught. Even then, you'll never be trusted again. Lying never ever pays off.

Know Your Audience

By audience, I mean anyone you're speaking to. Sierra Leadership explained it well:

> Once you know your audience, you are in a better position to fully connect with them. But importantly, this doesn't mean abandoning your core message. The task becomes to communicate your message, staying true to what you think and believe, but conveying it using language that speaks to them.[55]

Describe Problems Clearly

> *If I had an hour to solve a problem, I'd spend 55 minutes thinking about the problem and 5 minutes thinking about solutions.*[56]
> —*Albert Einstein*

Thinking about the problem in a way that leads to solving the problem is time well spent. The grids in this chapter are good examples of how to think about problems in a productive way.

Let's take a look at Paula's grid. She's indicated that she will speak with her boss about her concerns. One aspect of Paula's personality that I like and respect so much is the passion she shows for her work. But any strength can become a weakness if overdone.

When Paula is upset, she tends to do a verbal download of her concerns and it sounds like this: "This is a problem! Joe wants me to do x and such and such is due and that conflicts with the timing of such and such and Cindy wants such and such and there's no way that we can do that and Bob needs such and such and this other project that we have is in jeopardy and we can't get it done!"

Paula's manager likely feels overwhelmed and at a loss for how to help. Her manager needs to understand the problem(s), so that they can work together on a solution. Here are the steps that Paula should take:

- Calm down
- Gather her thoughts
- Convey her concerns thoughtfully

I used to tell my team that I could be most helpful to them if they would clearly state the problem they're trying to solve. I also wanted them to think about the root cause of their problem as well as possible solutions. The reason I asked them to think about these things is that I wanted them to slow down and look at the problem more objectively.

Sometimes just stepping back from a problem gives your brain a chance to catch up with your emotions. Most problems aren't insurmountable when viewed with a clear mind. Take a breath when you're upset—I promise it helps.

Let's look at a tool that helps with problem-solving called the 5 Whys.

The 5 Whys

There are a variety of YouTube videos showing how this tool is used if you learn more effectively via video. Here's how I have used the tool for Paula:

I dread going to work because I have too much to do and I don't feel I'll ever catch up. (This is the feeling Paula expressed in her grid)

Why? I've been given way too much work to do.

Why? People from across the business are asking me to help them and I don't know how to say "no."

Why? They know that somehow I always manage to get things done no matter what so they come to me.

Why? I don't want to disappoint anyone, so I am working night and day to finish everything.

Why? If I disappoint someone, they'll think I'm incompetent and I might lose my job.

The final "why" for Paula reveals that she's afraid of losing her job. No one wants to lose their job, but it's unhealthy to let that fear consume you. Paula's fear drives her to accept unattainable goals and creates expectations from others that she'll get the job done no matter what. She comes through more times than not, but she is sacrificing her authentic self and her health in doing so.

Paula could lose her job despite her strong performance. It happens all the time, and it happened in 2020 to many people who did great work. The best defense is a good offense. Know your worth, save as much money as you can, always be open to other opportunities, and keep learning and growing. Those steps are all within your control.

Whether someone decides to fire you isn't something you can control by doing anything other than doing your best work and following your company's rules.

Paula's fear isn't logical given her exceptional performance, but it's a genuine fear for her that impacts her life and emotions in very real ways.

The PIN Discussion Model

I created a simple model that helps you describe problems and ask for help solving them. I call it the PIN Discussion Model. Sharing the problem, information and your needs is a straightforward and effective approach for most discussions.

I've included the specific words that Paula could use to speak with her manager:

Problem (State this clearly and concisely)

- I'm concerned about my ability to get my work done on time and with the level of quality that is important.

Information (Think of this as evidence of the problem)

- I've prepared a list of all the requests that I've received and the key deliverables.
- I've prioritized the deliverables based on my understanding of your priorities as I understand them.
- I've also identified the key challenges and have listed them for you.

- I don't want to disappoint you or the team, but it's not possible for me to complete all this work by the time requested with our existing resources.

What I Need From You

- I would appreciate your review of these deliverables and advice on how we can move forward.

Summary

The approach I've presented is professional and shows that Paula has thought about the problem, taken ownership of it, and is seeking help from her manager.

Most managers genuinely want to help. The PIN Discussion Model helps them understand what's happening and what you feel is needed to solve the problem.

If you have a manager who is incapable of or unwilling to help you, you might receive a reaction like this: "You're here to solve problems—you tell me what you think we should do." If this is the response you receive, then I'd respond by describing what you can do and when you can do it. Then deliver on your commitment.

Paula and I used to work together. I never minded if she needed to vent. In fact, everyone I've ever worked with has vented at some time or another. Heck, I've vented as well! It's normal to be frustrated at work and healthy to have someone to speak with about your frustrations. Just choose your confidants carefully.

Paula needed more than someone to listen to her frustrations. She was losing sleep and rightfully dreaded coming to work. She wasn't doing the things that mattered to her at home or at work. When I worked with her, I couldn't help her unless I genuinely understood the challenges she was facing. A verbal download didn't help me in that endeavor. This is what I mean by knowing your audience.

Make it your business to understand how your manager wants you to communicate. Ask them what works for them. I've addressed communicating effectively with your manager, but the approach can be used with anyone else.

Watch Your Language

Have you ever been in a room with someone who was tossing out F-bombs like crazy and people were clearly uncomfortable? Don't let that someone be you.

I worked for Tom, who I described as being incredibly authentic earlier in the book. One observation that I made about Tom was that he never swore. I would watch his face when others swore in his presence and I could see the tiniest wince when they did. I never swore in front of him.

Even if someone you work with swears a lot, decide if that's a part of your authenticity that's important to show at work and whether your workplace has policies regarding swearing.

I'm someone who swears to lighten an unpleasant situation. As I reflect on my career, I wish I wouldn't have sworn at work as much as I did. I didn't swear in front of everyone, but swearing isn't reflective of my authentic self. I don't know why I did that and it's a regret. WTF?!

We'll talk more about intention later in the book. With the awareness that I swore too much and it's not really "me," I've stopped swearing for the most part and it feels good.

Be Deliberate When Presenting

Knowing your audience is especially important when presenting. Prepare your commentary and stay on point. Never swear when presenting and avoid making spur-of-the moment jokes—they usually don't go over well or have the impact you desire.

I attended a conference a while back and the presenter was someone who has written some successful books and is viewed as an expert in leadership. I don't know if it was nerves or if he felt he needed to lighten up the room, but he went off topic and "joked" about someone beating his wife. His presentation ended with a thud. A seasoned presenter shouldn't make that kind of mistake. Neither should the rest of us.

Share Personal Information Thoughtfully

Sharing information about yourself is important to being authentic at work. Decide what you want to share and with whom and consider the risks of doing so.

Lisa Rosh and Lynn Offermann offer the following point of view:

> But the honest sharing of thoughts, feelings, and experiences at work is a double-edged sword: Despite its potential benefits, self-disclosure can backfire if it's hastily conceived, poorly timed, or inconsistent with cultural or organizational norms—hurting your reputation, alienating employees, fostering distrust, and hindering teamwork.[57]

An executive I worked with previously told me that he never had a conversation at work that wasn't "deliberate." I took that as a cue that I should be deliberate as well. He would share some things about himself, such as the birth of a grandchild or that he had just returned from a great vacation, but generally he was a private person. We worked with each other for years, but I followed his lead and didn't share overly personal things with him. This worked well for us.

One word of caution: a few times in my career I've seen people share something personal about themselves as a means of giving someone a false sense of trust. Once they've reeled them in, the other person shares something personal and then the unscrupulous person uses that information against them when convenient to do so. People like this usually get the reputation they deserve, and they're not trusted.

Don't Gossip

A simple definition of gossip is to discuss something about someone who isn't present. It's human nature to talk about people, but it should be done sparingly and only with people you have a deep, trusting relationship with—otherwise you risk someone telling someone else what you shared and then having to defend yourself. Will it have been worth it to you to be in that position?

I worked with someone who was in a senior level position in HR who seemed to enjoy gossiping. This was a red flag to me because as a rule, HR professionals avoid gossiping entirely because they serve as an example to others. This person would often tell me things that members of her team or other employees had shared with her in confidence. There was no reason for her to tell me what she told me, and it made me uncomfortable.

Here's what I learned from those encounters: I would never tell her anything about myself or anyone else that I didn't want shared.

Researchers at the University of California Riverside found that the average person gossips about fifty-two minutes a day. Gossip falls into three categories: neutral (observations about people that aren't positive or negative), negative/malicious, and positive/flattering. The majority of gossip (75 percent) is neutral, 15 percent is negative, and 10 percent is positive.[58]

If someone is gossiping about others, they're probably gossiping about you as well. My advice is to avoid gossip entirely.

Admit to Mistakes

I used to have a boss who always said, "Do it to yourself before someone does it to you." This is good advice when it comes to admitting to mistakes. Listen, everyone makes mistakes and the best thing you can do is to let your manager know when you've made one before they find out from someone else.

Julie was a young woman on my team who handled payroll. First, payroll is a difficult and often thankless job and it's prone to error. Julie was great about letting me know when something went wrong. As she recalls, "It was always better to give you a heads up before the shit hit the fan!" Well said!

Her approach to talking to her manager about a problem was to describe the following:

- The error
- Who or what was impacted
- Any additional details such as financial impact if known
- Why it happened
- Possible solutions
- Why it won't happen again

I asked Julie how she became so adept at admitting mistakes. She said, "I used to be super uncomfortable owning my mistakes. I would go into my boss's office and I'd kind of work up to the problem rather than starting with what happened. I can literally picture her saying, 'Just spit it out!' She wanted me to tell her the problem first and then let her ask questions. I didn't realize that it sounded like I was making excuses instead of giving her the information she needed. And she always told me that if I was going to bring a problem, she wanted to hear my thoughts on a solution."

When you're new in your career, it's tough to admit to mistakes. Everyone makes mistakes sometimes so learn from them, don't repeat them and move on.

Express Your Feelings Thoughtfully

This book is about being authentic. Feelings play a huge role in our authenticity. Nonetheless, sharing your feelings at work should be done thoughtfully. Everyone feels anger, confusion, frustration, joy (I hope), and a host of other emotions at work, but how we share them matters. When it comes to feelings, one shouldn't "try to 'manage' or suppress them, but if you can pause long enough to consider how to communicate your feelings, you and your coworkers will always be better off."[59]

You know yourself and what sets you off right? Here's what I know about myself: I am uncomfortable with anger. When I see someone who is angry and they start yelling, finger-pointing and the like, I think, "Wow, that person has lost all control!" As the child of alcoholics, losing control is incredibly uncomfortable for me. In general, it's uncomfortable for most people, especially at work.

I don't communicate in the heat of the moment because I'm uncomfortable doing so. Once words are said, you can't take them back. Take some time to cool off and then, if you really have a problem with someone, communicate with that person directly. Tell them what is troubling to you and ask them to help you understand why they did what they did.

You can use the PIN Discussion Model as a guide for your commentary. People will respect you for using this approach.

Show Empathy

Merriam-Webster defines empathy as "the action of understanding, being aware of, being sensitive to, and vicariously experiencing the feelings, thoughts and experience of another of either the past or present without having the feelings, thoughts, and experience fully communicated in an objectively explicit manner." I'd define it as walking a mile in another's shoes.

As humans, we're all imperfect. When you allow yourself to accept yourself, flaws and all, you can do the same with others. I think you can't really be authentic unless you accept others' authenticity as well. The reason I say this is that authenticity is the result of knowing and accepting yourself, and with that experience, you can see others' humanity as well. Not every hill is worth dying on, so as my mom would say, "Pick your battles with care."

Do What You Say You'll Do

Can you be authentic and never keep your word? Absolutely! But would anyone in their right mind choose to do that? If you genuinely want to succeed at work and in your relationships, make commitments with care and then keep them.

Everyone has their unique way of keeping track of commitments. I used to keep journals at work so I could keep tabs on discussions and things I needed to complete. It worked for me. If you don't have a foolproof method of tracking your work or promises to others, talk to someone who excels in that area and learn their method.

If you realize you forgot to do something you promised to someone, let them know as soon as possible and apologize. It happens to everyone at one time or another. Again, if you made the commitment with every intention of keeping it and then failed to do so, you will authentically feel bad about not keeping your word and it will show when you let someone know.

Be Thoughtful About Workplace Romance

As a former head of HR, I will tell you that I think workplace romances are risky propositions and have the potential to cause harm to those involved as well as the company. Understand the policies at your workplace and consider the impact to your credibility before you proceed.

Learn to Say "No" More Often

In *The Success Principles*, Jack Canfield writes that it's important to "give yourself time to think it over before making any new agreements. I write the word 'no' in yellow highlighter on all my calendar pages as a way to remind myself to really consider what else I'll have to give up if I say yes to something new. It makes me pause and think before I add another commitment to my life."[60]

Express Gratitude

I keep a rock with the word "gratitude" on it on my desk at all times. I have so much to be grateful for and I never want to lose sight of this fact. If someone is helpful to you or teaches you an important lesson, be grateful for it and thank the person that did so. The simple words "thank you" mean so much and we often take them for granted, but they mean so much to those who hear these words.

It's more challenging to be grateful for painful lessons. While you don't need to thank people who have treated you poorly, be grateful for the learning that resulted and use it to make decisions about where you want to work and with whom.

When you wake up in the morning, say "thank you" to the universe. There's a book called *The Five-Minute Journal* that helps you to think about what you're grateful for and how you can make the day great. I highly recommend it if you want to focus more on gratitude.

Love Yourself

Last, but not least, the most basic aspect of being authentic is to love yourself. Treat yourself as you'd treat your most cherished friend. If you make a mistake, forgive yourself. Don't tolerate mistreatment by anyone. Look in the mirror and allow yourself to be proud of the person you see in front of you. This is my deepest hope for everyone.

Key Takeaways

- The grid is an effective tool to help you understand your feelings, fears, and strategy for bringing more of your authentic self to work.
- The PIN discussion framework helps you in communicating problems and what's needed to solve them. It's an effective framework for talking to your manager or others by (a) stating the problem, (b) providing supporting information, and (c) asking for what you need to succeed.
- Incorporating the authenticity basics in your daily work will enhance your authenticity.

Mom, dad, my brother Daniel and me at 6 months old

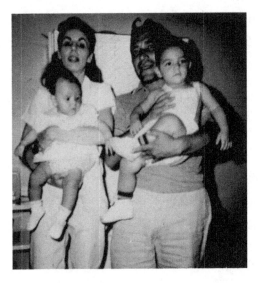

My first school picture. I loved school so much.

Still together nearly forty years later

Mom, Tom, Dad and Me 1984

The honor of my lifetime is to be
these beautiful girls' mother

My pal Buster. He spent every moment
with me as I wrote this book

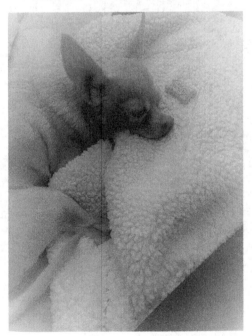

6 CONFLICT, COURAGE, CURIOSITY, AND COMPASSION

So far, we've talked about what authenticity is, what it looks like, ways to know it's missing at work, and some basic actions that will move your authenticity forward.

Now it's time to dig deeper into the tough stuff: conflict, courage, curiosity, and compassion. There's a reason this entire chapter is devoted to these concepts; they can cause great discomfort, disruption, and confusion.

Humans are wired to seek pleasure and avoid pain. If conflict feels painful to us, we will do all we can to avoid it. If one is wired such that compassion is painful, the tendency would be to avoid that emotion as well. I wish pain were unavoidable, but it isn't. If it's any consolation, we often learn more from pain than pleasure.

Emotions are complex to say the least. We usually don't just feel one emotion, but instead have many feelings all seemingly competing with one another to find their proper place in our psyches. Each of us grapples with our emotions and feelings in our own unique ways.

I've lost countless hours of sleep trying to understand and resolve conflict through the lens of compassion. What I mean by that is that there were times when I would feel anger, frustration, disappointment and perhaps sadness, but compassion always seemed to take the lead. Processing how to get to compassion from being really ticked off wasn't a deliberate requirement for me, but that is where my true self takes me when dealing with conflict. What's your normal approach?

The emotions and behaviors we'll discuss in this chapter challenge us to show up as our authentic selves during challenging times. They test us to either be who we truly are or to lose that person and be someone we're not. The choice isn't always easy.

Conflict

Conflict arises in every relationship yet most of us aren't skilled in managing it. We want to think that we are addressing conflict in our relationships, but I think it's safe to say that what we really do is avoid conflict or pretend it doesn't exist.

The word conflict comes from the early 15th century from Old French *conflit* and originally from Latin *conflictus* "a striking together".[61]

When I read the etymology of the word "conflict," I thought it interesting that it means a "striking together." Conflict feels that way doesn't it? We often use the term "bumping heads" to describe conflict. No one wants to intentionally bump heads but because we all come to relationships with our own unique life stories and perspectives, it's inevitable.

In some ways, 2020 has taught me so much about this concept of "striking together". As I look at the political landscape, I've seen conflict like I've never seen before both personally and across the country. People say things on social media that they'd never say to someone's face. Some of us are looking at people we genuinely love and wondering how in the world we could see things so differently. We are bumping heads but not solving much at all. Sigh.

We all have conflict that's within us and conflict that comes to us from or because of others. I don't know about you, but I have had many internal conflicts and they've been more challenging and disruptive to me than the conflicts I've had with others. Maybe that's because I live with myself twenty-four hours a day.

When we're conflicted, it can feel like you're standing at a fork in the road and weighing the options of taking one direction vs. another. Sometimes both directions make sense, sometimes neither makes sense, and sometimes one path is the clear path forward but may be more challenging or painful than you'd hope or are ready to tackle. See what I mean?

According to the book, *Optimal Outcomes: Free Yourself From Conflict at Work, at Home and in Life*, "conflict is inevitable. A healthy amount of conflict is part of a well-functioning life, team, organization, or society. However, recurring conflict makes it hard to be present or contribute the way you'd like to the people and world around you."[62]

Internal Conflict

Cognitive dissonance is the term used to describe conflicting feelings within yourself. An example of cognitive dissonance is when someone knows that smoking is deadly but does it anyway. I know that exercise is good for me, but I really dislike it and usually sit for hours at a time at my desk. I'm sure you have internal debates with yourself as well. We all have cognitive dissonance.

Jenna is someone whose cognitive dissonance made working with and knowing her a real challenge. On one hand, she talked passionately in meetings about how much she cared about people, health, working collaboratively, and being kind. I believe she meant what she said, but it was obvious to me that she wasn't really applying her philosophies to her own life. She looked unwell and stressed.

Unfortunately, when Jenna is stressed, her cognitive dissonance is on full display and it's not clear what genuinely matters to her. One day she says one thing, the next day there's a sudden change of heart and it's as if the previous discussion never occurred. Have you ever worked with someone like this? I'm reminded of a line from the play Hamilton where Hamilton says to Aaron Burr, "If you stand for nothing, Burr, what'll you fall for?"[63]

There were times when it looked as if Jenna was having an argument with herself in her own mind as she weighed which direction she should take. Instead of the warm, caring person, she claims to be, a dark side emerges. She can be abrupt, distrustful of others' intentions, and directive rather than the warm, collaborative person she claims to be.

In the article "Oprah's Life Lesson from Maya Angelou: When People Show You Who They Are, Believe Them," Winfrey says, "When a person says to you, 'I'm selfish,' or 'I'm mean' or 'I am unkind,' believe them." She goes on to say that she amended Maya Angelou's famous quote so that it became "When people show you who they are, believe them *the first time*."[64]

Jenna's flip-flopping was confusing to me. She was a seasoned pro and seasoned pros know that sometimes you must change course if you're not getting the results that you expected. It happens all the time, but Jenna didn't just change course, she changed personas.

I wanted to help her not only because she was a colleague, but because I genuinely cared about her as a person. I could see that she was under significant pressure and that stress was impacting her health. I spoke with her many times and acknowledged her challenges, expressed concern and empathy.

I learned over time that Jenna wouldn't likely ever get to a place of complete trust. We'd have a warm, heart-to-heart conversation about the best way to work together, but it was always just a matter of time before she'd again resort to the confusing behavior. Rinse, repeat. I gave up trying.

I want to be clear here that what was so confusing and disappointing about Jenna is that she presented such conflicting sides of the values she espoused that it wasn't clear who she was or what she valued.

So why did I share this story? You're going to work with people who have internal conflicts like Jenna and those conflicts may directly impact you. You can't control other people's internal conflicts, but you can control how you communicate with them.

The approach I tried with Jenna was to let her know that I was concerned and wanted to collaborate with her and help if possible, but I couldn't fix whatever it was that caused her to be so conflicted at work. Nonetheless, I worked well enough with Jenna, but if she would've allowed herself to truly be the collaborative person that she said she wanted to be, we could've done great work together. That didn't happen.

What are your internal conflicts? Do you ever catch yourself espousing values that you know you're not living up to yourself? Make note of them and spend some time resolving these conflicts within yourself. If the internal conflict feels like it's starting to get out of hand or consuming your thoughts, please seek professional help.

External Conflict

External conflict involves others. According to the book *Resolving Conflicts at Work: Ten Strategies for Everyone on the Job*, employees spend 20-80% of their working hours trying to resolve or contain conflict.[65]

Most of these conflicts are unnecessary, are easily solved and are attributed to miscommunication, unclear roles and responsibilities, false expectations, or poor leadership. Sometimes the conflict is chronic and at other times it's easily resolved. Let's look at what I mean.

Chronic Conflict

This kind of conflict "goes deeper into the structures, systems, processes, and relationships in the workplace; the nature of conflict, the culture of conflict within organizations; and the ways work is organized, compensated, processed, and acknowledged."[66]

Chronic conflict is tough to resolve because there's something inherent to the company's culture that allows the conflict to exist in the first place. Correcting it means that a more significant change must occur.

Sometimes these issues never get resolved because the people in leadership roles don't have the ability or desire to resolve the issues. I used to have a manager who treated his team a little bit like a father would treat his children. He wanted everyone on his team to play nice and get along. He didn't want to be put in a position to have to resolve issues because he didn't want to have to "pick a side." It's a tough situation to be in if you're not able to change things, but you're nonetheless impacted by the dysfunction caused by them.

Managers are responsible for resolving matters that can't be resolved without their advice. Sometimes the manager is the cause of the conflict but might not realize this is the case. Eventually someone on the team must discuss the matter with the manager or it'll linger.

For example, let's say that you're in a situation where the reporting structure for your department doesn't make sense. You have two managers who don't speak with each other and both are talking to you about each other and confusing your assignments. On the next page I discuss a way to help with this type of discussion.

The Intentional Compassionate Conflict Model

Here's an approach that can be used to discuss this situation with your manager(s). I call this the Intentional Compassionate Conflict Model. I've included sample commentary to help you see how this model would work in the situation I laid out above:

1. **State your intention**: My intention in speaking with you is to help us be more productive.

2. **Describe what is happening**: In the last few weeks I've received countless confusing assignments and messages. (Give specific examples).

3. **Describe how you were impacted**: It's unclear to me which assignments are the priorities and it's causing confusion in terms of what work needs to be completed first.

4. **Describe your feelings**: I feel caught between the two of you and don't think this is a healthy situation. I want to help both of you succeed but this dynamic isn't working well.

5. **Ask for an explanation:** Can you help me understand your perspective?

6. **Listen and clarify anything you don't understand:** So, what I hear you say is... (repeat your understanding of the explanation).

7. **Describe what will make it better or right**: Can we all meet once a week to discuss the priorities? This will help me get to know you both better and will help us work better as a team.

8. **Express gratitude**: Thanks for your time; I appreciate that you worked through this with me.

Before we leave the model, I want to point out the importance of Steps 1 and 7. Step 1, where you state your intention, requires that you think about your reason for discussing the situation. Taking the time to think about the situation helps you put things in perspective and gain confidence in speaking with others about what you're experiencing.

Step 7 includes the question that I promise will serve you well in virtually every conflict. The simple question "what will make it better?" is one I've asked hundreds of people and I'm usually surprised that they haven't thought about what a positive solution would look like. They've usually just focused on their grievances.

If you find yourself in a situation where someone is troubled by something you've done, use this simple question with them as well: "What will make it better?" You'll be pleasantly surprised by how much this simple question can enable a productive conversation.

Unnecessary and Avoidable Conflict

We're not taught how to handle conflict effectively. As a result, sometimes minor irritants take on a life of their own and cause a disproportionate amount of conflict. Some of the easily solved conflicts at work that I've seen are due to the following:

- Feeling that you do more and/or better work than someone else
- Feeling left out or not appreciated
- Thinking that someone is receiving favorable treatment
- Disagreeing about process

- Different communication styles or misunderstanding what someone said
- Being confused about roles and responsibilities
- Needless competition
- Feeling that someone is not appreciating your privacy
- Someone's workspace or behavior is annoying
- Having meaningful differences in values

Once you understand the cause of the conflict, you can decide if it's worth it to you to resolve it or if it will only make matters worse if you say something. Here are some things to consider before engaging with someone else.

What Stories Are You Telling Yourself?

Is it possible you're telling yourself a story about the conflict that may not be true? Some stories impact a relationship and others don't.

Let's say that Joe and Bob are working on a project. Bob is the lead. Joe asks some questions about some of Bob's suggestions. Bob automatically thinks "why the hell is he asking about that? He must think I'm an idiot. That guy is trying to get my job!" Bob has convinced himself that these feelings are true, and he no longer trusts Joe as a result. This kind of thing happens all the time and it's so unfortunate. If Bob keeps assuming the worst about Joe and they don't have a heart-to-heart discussion, their relationship will be ruined. All because of a lie that Bob told himself. Maybe this is what happens to Jenna as well.

There's a host of stories we might make up. These stories might sound like "my boss is trying to make my life difficult,"

"Ed is trying to show me up because he wants my job," "they don't think I'm capable of doing the work" or "she thinks she's smarter than all of us." You get the idea.

Take a moment and consider if you're telling yourself a story about someone with whom you experience conflict.

My advice here is to ask yourself if it's possible you've misunderstood something and made up a story that may not be true. Would you consider talking to the person and trying to understand their point of view about what's causing conflict? Sometimes it helps and if it doesn't at least you tried.

Reasons to Avoid Conflict

I used to have a boss who would ask "is this a hill to die on?" when I was grappling with whether I should engage in conflict. Most of the time "it" wasn't. As you think about engaging in conflict, consider if it's worth it to you. Sometimes it isn't.

If you feel the conflict is trivial or that addressing it isn't as important as keeping the peace, then just let it go. For me, someone's annoying habits probably fall in the "not worth it" category since everyone does something that's annoying.

Reasons to Address Conflict

If someone else's behavior is impacting you, you should address the matter with the person(s) involved. Sometimes people talk to everyone except the person directly involved. This isn't helpful. Take some time to think about what's troubling you and then engage with the other person.

Let's say that Patti is working with David on a project. David dropped the ball a few times and Patti had to work tirelessly to meet the deadline. Patti knows that David is a talented person who can do the work, but he has let her down and she's starting to resent him.

Let's apply the **Intentional Compassionate Conflict Model** to this situation:

1. **State your intention:** I want us to be the great team that we've always been.

2. **Describe what happened**: Last week you dropped the ball quite a few times and you didn't do the work you promised you'd do.

3. **Describe how you were impacted**: I had to work late three days last week to do your part and now I'm behind on my other projects.

4. **Describe your feelings**: David, I'm starting to feel that I can't count on you to do your part of the work to complete our projects. We've got two more projects coming our way and I can't do the work alone.

5. **Ask for an explanation:** Can you help me understand what happened?

6. **Listen and clarify anything you don't understand.**

7. **Describe what will make it better or right**: I think it will help if we review our responsibilities together to ensure we can keep our commitments. Let's agree to communicate when there's a problem. If we have a problem going forward with each other, we will talk about it right away.

8. **Express gratitude:** I'm glad we could talk about this. Thank you!

Patti described how she's feeling, the impact of David not doing his work and her concerns about the work that will be assigned to them in the future.

Do you also see what Patti did here? She asked David to help her understand what happened (Step 5) and she stopped to listen (Step 6). Listening is such an important step because it is the only way that Patti can help David feel heard. Sometimes when we are supposed to be listening, we are instead trying to come up with our next line. Listening means that we aren't trying to fill in the blanks for the other person. We are listening with intention—the intention to understand the other person's point of view.

Patti learned that David is going through a divorce and he's struggling personally. David apologized for letting her down and said he will communicate better with her going forward.

Before they close out the conversation, Patti needs to be clear about what she needs from him. As described in Step 7, she tells him what will make things right. She thanks David and repeats their agreement about how to work better together going forward.

Conflict Styles

The Intentional Compassionate Conflict Model I shared can be useful no matter who you're speaking with or their conflict style. Taking the time to understand your feelings and understanding your audience will help you prepare for a productive conversation.

In the book *Overcome Conflict Through the Power of Samemindedness*, Randal Gilmore outlines four conflict styles: Gladiator, Prisoner of War, Politician, and Barista.[67]

Gladiator

This type of person is high in assertiveness and low in cooperation. They will fight to the death to win. They're not empathetic and they destroy relationships.

In the story I shared about David and Patti, if David was a Gladiator, he might not have shared his personal situation and said that Patti was the one who took on the project so she should do the work. Or he might not have been open to having a conversation at all. It happens.

In my view, this kind of person generally doesn't last too long in an organization because others won't cooperate with them and no one can do everything alone.

If you're a Gladiator, has this style served you well? If you've been successful with this style, you've been unusually lucky. I assure you this will negatively impact your career at some point, especially if you aspire to advance in the organization.

I've worked with a Gladiator before. He was a thorn in everyone's side who kept moving from position to position until his reputation was irreparable, leaving him with no option but to leave.

Tips for dealing with Gladiators: Be direct and fact-based with them. State your view of the conflict using the Intentional Compassionate Conflict Model. If they are more senior than you, speak with your manager and ask for advice and support in solving the conflict.

Prisoner of War

I'm not fond of this label, but this person is high in cooperation and low in assertiveness. They can act as if they have no rights and they often give in to others. They will settle for a lose/win situation (they lose, others win) and their needs won't be met.

In the story of David and Patti above, if Patti was the Prisoner of War, she might not say anything to David. She'd do the work and stew about it. She might even let David take credit for work that he didn't do.

If you're a Prisoner of War, work to understand why this is your conflict style. If you're new in your career, this may be your approach because you may feel that you must cooperate and you're not yet comfortable being assertive. Been there!

However, as you grow in your career and strengthen your authenticity, you won't feel comfortable always giving in to others. In other words, the more you know yourself and what's important to you, the less you're willing to just go along with everything that comes your way.

Tips for dealing with Prisoners of War: Convey to them that you want them to work with you to truly solve the conflict. You don't want them to just give in but to participate in the solution.

Politician

This person's behavior is between a Gladiator and a Prisoner of War. They compromise such that everyone gives up something so there are no losers, but there aren't any real winners either.

If David were a politician, maybe he'd apologize and say he'll try harder next time but not make a real commitment. If Patti is the Politician, she might just take him at his word, not ask for a commitment, and move on to the next project.

If you're a Politician, challenge yourself to understand what you really want and then don't let yourself compromise it away.

Tips for dealing with Politicians: Make sure you convey what is important to you and not up for compromise. Ask the politician what's important for them that they don't think should be compromised as well.

Barista

This style is high in assertiveness and cooperation. Just like a real-life barista, this person listens well and works to meet everyone's needs. Baristas are creative and they strive for samemindedness in that they work through conflict without blowing up the relationship, communicating what's important to others and why, motivating opponents to change their minds and going beyond compromise.

The Barista style is one that is well-suited to those who wish to be viewed as being collaborative and authentic. It may not be your "normal" style, but don't we all want to know and work with people who make us feel that our opinions matter?

This style takes time to learn and refine. If this isn't your go-to style, look around your workplace and find the person who you feel exhibits this style. Learn from watching what they do and build your expertise gradually by doing more of what they do on a regular basis.

Can you be more Barista-like in your interactions with others?

Tips for dealing with Baristas: Enjoy working with them—they're rare!

You don't have to remember the labels, but it does help to understand the general descriptions outlined above. Knowing the styles will help you manage your own behavior as well as conflict with others.

Courage

It takes courage just to be human. In fact, if we thought too much about how much courage it takes to face some of our days, we'd never get out of bed. But what is courage at work? According to the article "Courage at Work: Why Removing the Fear Barrier Increases Cross-Cultural Corporate Success," courage at work often shows up in personal ways.[68]

Here are a few personal ways that courage shows up according to the article:

• Admitting a mistake to a superior

• Making a client aware of problems with a faulty product

• Stepping down in the face of an inappropriate handling of a workplace situation

- Giving credit to others when it would be more advantageous to claim it for yourself

- Holding yourself accountable to the same standards you apply to everyone else

The moments where I've been most courageous have been those when I've stood up to anyone when I observed decisions or actions that were against my values and/or the company's values. If you encounter these moments, you'll know it because speaking up will be so important to you that you'll be willing to lose or quit your job over them.

Another way courage shows up is by admitting that you were wrong. It takes courage to make it right, but I promise you that unless you do make it right, you'll carry the weight of your prideful position with you every day. It's a heavy load. Apologize and mean it and then forgive yourself.

The Intentional Compassionate Conflict Model helps you think about your concerns and how to communicate them. That approach works in most situations. If you need help, talk to a trusted friend, advisor, or someone in HR.

Curiosity

> *Listen with curiosity. Speak with honesty. Act with integrity. The greatest problem with communication is we don't listen to understand. We listen to reply. When we listen with curiosity, we don't listen with the intent to reply. We listen for what's behind the words.*[69]
>
> —Roy T. Bennett, *The Light in the Heart*

Some of my favorite people are endlessly curious about everything, especially human behavior. You're curious too or you wouldn't be reading this book. Thank you so much for doing so.

How do you satisfy your curiosity? Reading is one way of course. What about talking with others or attending conferences? I love podcasts. There is an endless supply of information available to us, but unless we have a genuine desire to understand any given situation or topic, availability is irrelevant.

In the article "Wonder, Curiosity, and Openness," Ellie Ballentine suggests that when we're confronted by something or someone, stepping into wonder can help.[70]

Imagine starting a sentence with "I wonder" as opposed to "I know." Your thinking takes on a different tone when you say, "I wonder what's going on" or "I wonder what's happened between us" or "I wonder if we could get to a better answer by looking at this situation together."

Curiosity is powerful. Sometimes we can't move forward because we think we are "right" and, of course, the other person is "wrong." Sometimes we get caught up in "winning," but fail to realize that the victory came at the expense of someone else's feelings, credibility, etc. Sometimes we're so angry or hurt we aren't thinking logically.

Sometimes we are afraid of not knowing it all, aren't we? After all, the people who get rewarded the most seem to be those who act as if they've got all the answers so why not join the crowd? Trust me, the people who seem to know it all, don't.

Staying curious will not only increase your knowledge, but it'll increase your authenticity as well. People like and appreciate being genuinely collaborated with and being heard.

Having the willingness to step back to see another point of view will result in your growing as a person and a professional. You may still believe that you're right, but you will be better informed by stepping into curiosity.

Compassion

If you were magically given the power to know your colleagues' life stories, I guarantee that some of those stories would drop you to your knees. Instead of being upset that they didn't get a report done on time, you'd praise them for going through all they've gone through in their life and making it to where they are today.

I've seen people come to work who have lost loved ones, suffered from domestic violence, are dealing with alcohol or drug addiction, been told by their spouse that they're no longer loved, are battling cancer and know they're going to die and so much more. They still come to work, and their intention is to do the best work they can do.

What if you knew the person sitting next to you at work was going to die tomorrow? Would you treat them with deep respect today? I imagine you would. Would it matter that the report is an hour later than you hoped it would be? Probably not.

From time to time, remind yourself that the people you work with are human beings. We're all imperfect, but we're doing the best we can. When I think about Jenna from earlier in the chapter, I feel deep compassion for her because I am sure she's hurting inside. That makes me sad.

In her best-selling book, *Rising Strong*, Brené Brown shared this about compassionate people: "Steve says his life is better when he assumes people are doing the best they can. I think he's right." She goes on to say "compassionate people ask for what they need. They say no when they need to, and when they say yes, they mean it."[71]

How about having compassion for yourself? In the article "Four Reasons Why Compassion Is Better for Humanity Than Empathy," Rasmus Hougaard writes that "having genuine compassion for others starts with having compassion for yourself."[72]

I agree with the author when he advises the reader to "stop criticizing yourself for what you could have done differently or better. Instead, cultivate self-talk that is positive."

Work is important, but people are more important and always will be. Treat them that way and treat yourself that way.

The Power of Forgiveness

Forgiving Others

At the core of compassion is forgiveness. As humans we inherently want to protect ourselves, so our instinct is to put up a wall (forever!) when people hurt us. The problem with doing that is that with every wall you erect, you limit your ability to let in love for yourself.

In an article called "The Power of Forgiveness," Tyler VanderWeele, co-director of the Initiative on Health, Religion, and Spirituality at Harvard's T. H. Chan School of Public

Health, says, "Forgiving a person who has wronged you is never easy, but dwelling on those events and reliving them over and over can fill your mind with negative thoughts and suppressed anger. Yet, when you learn to forgive, you are no longer trapped by the past actions of others and can finally feel free."[73]

Another article with the same title offers further insights by saying that "forgiveness means giving up the suffering of the past and being willing to forge ahead with far greater potential for inner freedom."[74]

Sometimes we carry the pain of wanting something other than what happened to have happened, but it's done! We can't change the past. More importantly, do we want to drag the past into our future as well?

Are you dragging around the weight of not forgiving someone? Is doing so serving you well? What would it take to forgive that person? I'm not saying that you must forget, but please consider forgiving whoever has hurt you.

I want to acknowledge that some pain in our lives is just too much to handle alone and forgiving may not be possible. If this is your situation, please seek professional help and support; it's just too much to carry alone. Big hug to you; I pray that you find peace.

Forgiving Yourself

The last thing I want to say about forgiveness is that it's also important to forgive yourself. There isn't a person on the planet who hasn't made mistakes. If you don't forgive yourself, you'll never be free to be yourself. Forgiving yourself means that you are sorry for your actions, learned from them and won't make the same mistake again. If you can't seem to forgive yourself for whatever it is that you've done, seek professional help to do so.

Newton's Third Law of Motion

Newton's third law of motion says that for every action in nature, there is an equal and opposite reaction. I'm not a physics scholar, but I love how this law applies to being compassionate. Oprah Winfrey explained this law beautifully in a YouTube video:[75]

> No matter what you do, the energy of what you do, what you say and, most important, the energy of who you are is going out into the world, into your home, into your relationships and that energy is always coming back to you. You are responsible for the energy that you are putting out into the world because that very energy (bam!) is coming right back to you every single time whether you believe it or not because it is law.
>
> I've seen it countless times in my lifetime. It's true.

This chapter felt intense to me. Was it the same for you? Visiting these feelings caused me to feel the weight of some of the hurts I've caused and received.

An authentic path doesn't mean that you won't experience or cause pain; it's inevitable that you will do so because that's what it means to be human. But the path will be authentically yours, not someone else's.

> *I am responsible for everything in my life. I am responsible for what I was. I am responsible for what I will become.*[76]
> —*David Viscott*

Key Takeaways

- We all grapple with internal and external conflict. Taking the time to understand what's causing it and using the Intentional Compassionate Conflict Model helps to resolve it in a straightforward, authentic way.

- Sometimes we tell ourselves stories that create conflict that exists only in our thoughts.

- Shifting your approach from "I know" to "I wonder" can be a powerful approach to understanding and resolving conflict.

- Having compassion for yourself and others frees us from feeling we must be perfect and allows for genuine, authentic relationships.

- Sometimes despite doing and saying the right things, conflict will not be resolved leaving you with only the satisfaction that you tried to improve the situation.

7 WHAT YOU STAND FOR AND WHY YOU'RE HERE

> *Once upon a time, there were three bricklayers. When asked, "What are you doing?" the first bricklayer replied: "I'm laying bricks." The second bricklayer was asked the same question. He answered: "I'm putting up a wall." The third bricklayer, when asked the question, "What are you doing?" responded, with pride in his voice: "I'm building a cathedral."*[77]

This story is often shared when discussing "purpose" and for good reason. There is honor and purpose in work, no matter what you do for a living. I think we're seeing just how true this is as we navigate the pandemic of 2020. The people who are cleaning hospitals are literally saving thousands of lives by doing their work with care. The difference between a thorough job and a lousy job could mean lost lives.

My mom was a housekeeper in a nursing home for over twenty years. She "slung a mop" all day long, all 90 pounds of her. What I loved about how she went about her work is that while she cleaned the rooms, she laughed and joked with the residents. If someone had asked her what her purpose was, I imagine she would've said something along the lines of (cue the Southern accent), "Hell, I don't know."

My mom was fulfilling a purpose and an important one at that. She was someone on whom the residents could rely for a shoulder to cry on or a good laugh after being told a dirty joke – this skill earned her the nickname "Evil," always said with a big smile. She brought joy to people in a really difficult situation. That's purpose! I'm proud of her.

Purpose reveals itself with the passage of time and it's deeply personal. When I was a child, my purpose seemed to be to bring harmony to my family. As I got older, I felt my purpose was to be a great wife and parent. More recently my purpose evolved to helping people find joy and fulfillment in their lives and work. The path I'm on has evolved in a way that makes great sense looking back.

My values have gained clarity, but they've been consistent my whole life. When you finish this chapter, you're going to understand and own key moments from your life, have a clear understanding of your values, and know your purpose. I'm excited and I hope you are as well. Prepare yourself. This can be intense. It was for me.

Going back to Viscott's quote from the beginning of the book: "The purpose of life is to discover your gift. The work of life is to develop it. The meaning of life is to give your gift away."[78]

The goal of this chapter is to help you achieve this powerful call to action. Before we get started, I wanted to share this quote by Emily McDowell—it's a good reminder that even if we feel lost or without purpose, our true self is still waiting to be reawakened:

> Finding yourself is not really how it works. You aren't a ten-dollar bill in last winter's coat pocket. You are also not lost. Your true self is right there, buried under cultural conditioning, other people's opinions, and inaccurate conclusions you drew as a kid that became your beliefs about who you are. 'Finding yourself' is actually returning to yourself. An unlearning, an excavation, a remembering of who you were before the world got its hands on you.[79]

McDowell was diagnosed with stage III cancer at age twenty-four. In a podcast with Kate Bowler, she laughed about how often well-intentioned people would inevitably talk to her about her diagnosis and share stories with her about other friends who died from cancer![80] I can't imagine how awful that would be to hear, but she learned to find humor in a terrible situation.

McDowell learned about the power of empathy from her diagnosis as well as the death of her best friend from cancer. She used what she learned from these life-changing events to create her own company. Emily McDowell & Friends (emilymcdowell.com) produces, among other things, amazing cards that help people connect with others in a humorous and empathetic way. One card on her website that I loved that explicitly addresses the situation described above reads as follows:

> When life gives you lemons, I won't tell you a story about my cousin's friend who died of lemons.

Kate Bowler has a wonderful podcast called 'Everything Happens with Kate Bowler." I learned about her as I was researching McDowell, because the two of them were featured in one of Bowler's podcasts called "Emily McDowell: There's No Good Card for That." Bowler was diagnosed with stage IV cancer at age thirty-five. She's experienced grueling procedures, but she desperately wants to live.

Bowler found purpose in her story. Her TED Talk called "Everything Happens for a Reason and Other Lies I've Loved" has been viewed over five million times and is one of the best I've seen. Be prepared to cry. I highly recommend watching it if you haven't already done so. She's written a book by the same title. She closes her TED Talk with the following:

> I see that the world is jolted by events that are wonderful and terrible, gorgeous, and tragic. I can't reconcile the contradiction, except that I am beginning to believe that these opposites do not cancel each other out. Life is so beautiful, and life is so hard.[81]

Life is indeed beautiful and hard. We all have pain and joy. Our stories matter, and I believe that each of us has a reason for being here. It's our life's work to understand why we're here and to share our gifts with others.

Discovering Your Five Pivotal Moments

In the article "Oprah: 5 Moments that Changed My Life," Winfrey talks about key moments in life: "There is not a moment that can't turn out to be useful later. Life is a huge classroom, and when you learn one lesson, you get to move on to the next one."[82]

As I read Winfrey's moments, I thought of the pivotal moments from my life. They are pivotal because they influenced my life significantly. As you will see, had some of my pivotal moments not happened, I am convinced that I would be an entirely different person.

On occasion I've been to events where young people come to listen to people tell their life stories. But isn't our own story important for us to own and appreciate? I think so. Your story has made you who you are and is key to who you will become. Your story matters.

Exercise 1: Five Pivotal Moments

I designed the following exercise to help you reflect upon five moments that are foundational to who you are today. Of course, you're not limited to five moments, so if adding a few more captures meaningful moments more effectively, please feel free to add them.

The matrix that follows captures moments from my life. As you can see, I've not only captured pivotal moments, but I've noted how I felt and how those moments have contributed to my strengths. I've also called out areas of discomfort that I still have to this day. Being mindful of what makes me uncomfortable helps me manage my emotions in a way that aligns with my purpose.

My Experiences	How I Felt	Gifts I've Developed as a Result (Areas of Discomfort, If Any)
When I was in 1st grade, I did my homework, and the class applauded because I wasn't known for doing my homework.	To this day, I can feel how proud I was that day. I can still see that little girl and the power of that moment. It changed my life forever.	I am known for doing my homework. I show up prepared. I get visibly irritated when others aren't prepared or try to fake their way through something.
My family lost our home to foreclosure, but we moved to a wonderful town where I flourished.	I was scared and embarrassed, but the move exposed me to healthy families, good teachers & studious peers.	I am disciplined with money and know that education changes lives for the better. I am a cautious risk-taker.
I've worked with amazing, smart people.	I've been inspired by so many people who have shown me the value of hard work, the joy that comes from pursuing excellence & the power of true collaboration.	I wanted to be like them and have worked hard to set the kind of example to others that was set for me. I worry that I will disappoint others.

I married my husband and had children.	I knew this was a leap of faith; I was young and hadn't seen many happy and fulfilling marriages at that point in my life. I wanted to raise children who would be great people (mission accomplished!).	I've learned to compromise & not take myself too seriously. I love unconditionally. I wish I were more spontaneous & that my kids never experienced pain, but I know it's an important part of lessons learned in life.
I watched my dad endure racism nearly every day.	I was angry, and my heart hurt for my dad.	Zero tolerance for racism. I won't back down when confronting racism.

Additional Notes from My Pivotal Moments

While my parents genuinely loved each other, they argued constantly. As a result, I do not respond well to raised voices. My inherent impression of people who raise their voices at work is that they are out of control and unable to problem-solve in a productive way. My impression doesn't make me right or wrong, but I am aware that I feel this way about "yellers and screamers." Not a fan.

As I revisited my five pivotal moments, I cried because I took time to *feel* what I felt in those moments. It was clear to me that some of the most painful moments of my life, while difficult to experience at the time, resulted in good things later in life.

If a bunch of first graders hadn't clapped for me in first grade, maybe I would never have been a great student. While it was a very painful event, if we hadn't lost our home to foreclosure we wouldn't have moved to a town where I flourished. If I hadn't worked with people who were so smart and great at their work, I might not have set such a high personal bar for achievement. Had I not gotten married to the man that I married, I wouldn't have had the family that has given me more joy than I can express. Those moments clearly changed my life.

Are you ready to dive into your story? What are the five pivotal moments of your life?

Take your time and think about moments that you believe changed your life. This may be painful for some of you, but those moments are part of who you are. I encourage you to seek help from a professional if an experience causes you emotional distress.

Your Five Pivotal Moments

Think back as far as you can and make note of the pivotal moments in your life in the grid below. You're not limited to five moments of course, but the goal is to capture those that were truly impactful to your life.

My Experiences	How I Felt	Gifts I've Developed as a Result (Areas of Discomfort, If Any)

Additional Notes from Your Pivotal Moments

Take some time to reflect upon other moments from your life that were important to your life and note them below.

Once you're done, read what you've written. Are you surprised by anything that you wrote? Did you go all the way back as far as you can remember? Can you see how you became "you" because of these experiences? Take it in and appreciate how you got to where you are today and the lessons you'll take with you as you fulfill your purpose.

I love the book *You Are a Badass* by Jen Sincero, the magnificent and oh-so-funny *New York Times* best-selling author. Her words are a great reminder of the importance of accepting and being ourselves.

> You are perfect. To think anything less is as pointless as a river thinking that it's got too many curves or that it moves too slowly or that its rapids are too rapid. Says who? You're on a journey with no defined beginning, middle or end. There you can be. This is why you're here. To shy away from who you truly are would leave the world you-less. You are the one and only one there is and ever will be. I repeat, you are the only one there is and ever will be. Do not deny the world its one and only chance to bask in your brilliance.
>
> We are all perfect in our own, magnificent fucked-up ways. Laugh at yourself. Love yourself and others. Rejoice in the cosmic ridiculousness.[83]

Sincero has a wonderful way with words. I highly recommend her books if you haven't already read them.

Values

The Cambridge Dictionary defines values as "the principles that help you to decide what is right and wrong, and how to act in various situations." I think this is a simple and helpful definition.

You can find lists of values online, but I hope you won't get too caught up in the words themselves because that'll drive you a little batty.

After all these years, I have learned that I have a values barometer and I bet you do as well. I'm a calm, laid-back person and I easily find common ground with others unless something bumps up against my personal values. When that happens, I turn into a lioness and won't back down no matter what.

I've learned this about myself because when I reflect on the moments at work that I've dug in my heels on something or when I've decided that someone isn't someone I care to engage with, it's always because it's clear that our values are completely different. For me, it's always about values. I'm going to guess that the same may be true for most humans. Keep this in mind as we proceed to Exercise 2.

Exercise 2: Identify Your Values

Let's use the work you did in Exercise 1 earlier in this chapter to find your values. Here's the process that I followed. First, I looked at the last column in Exercise 1. I translated some of the gifts/discomforts into one- or two-word descriptors. The values I picked up are the things that I know I care deeply about and have a strong reaction to when they're challenged.

Gifts I've Developed (last column in Exercise 1) and Areas of Discomfort (if any)	Values
I am known for doing my homework; I show up prepared. I get visibly irritated when others aren't prepared or try to fake their way through something.	Preparation Learning Honesty
I am disciplined with money and know that education changes lives for the better. I wish I were more comfortable taking risks.	Discipline Financial responsibility
I wanted to be like them and have worked hard to set the kind of example to others that they set for me. I worry that I will disappoint others.	Hard work
I've learned to compromise and not take myself too seriously. I love unconditionally and am grateful for my health so I can see them live their lives. I wish I were more spontaneous and that my kids never experienced pain although I know it's an important part of life.	Ability to compromise Love Fun and spontaneity
Zero tolerance for racism. I won't back down when confronting racism.	Respect for human beings

Looking at my completed matrix, here's what I value:

- Preparation
- Learning
- Honesty
- Discipline
- Financial responsibility

- Hard work
- The ability to compromise
- Love
- Fun and spontaneity
- Respect for human beings

We're not going for an all-inclusive list but a list that makes sense to you. When I look at my list, it rings true to me. You can have more or less than 10—they're your values.

Ok, now it's your turn to identify your values. Ready? Let's go!

My Values

Gifts I've Developed (last column in Exercise 1) and Areas of Discomfort (if any)	Values

Once you're done, ask yourself if the values you identified make sense to you. Do you demonstrate your values in your daily work? Are there some that you didn't realize were important to you? Would your friends and colleagues say that you demonstrate these values on a consistent basis?

Knowing your values and living up to them is one of the most important steps in knowing and being your authentic self. Your values represent what you stand for –they're *how* you'll bring your purpose to life.

We'll come back to this list as we proceed through the chapter.

Purpose

Finding your purpose is not easy because it evolves as you evolve and grow. I loved what Aaron McHugh says in his book *Fire Your Boss: Discover Work You Love Without Quitting Your Job*:

> Finding purpose and meaning is a lifelong pursuit requiring constant adjustment and course correction. Throughout life, we change and what used to turn our crank may not anymore, which means this life skill is a muscle you want to prioritize strengthening.

> Everyone loses the trail, drifts off course, and in seasons we can find ourselves disconnected and off purpose. The art of living well is building the awareness to detect when you feel you're living on purpose and when you are ever so slightly feeling off purpose.

You appreciate that discovering one life-sustaining, all answering purpose is way too complicated and riddled with challenges. Instead, you focus your attention and intentions toward living forward by paying careful attention to your values (e.g., "be a person of integrity") and your actions. You allow a lot of grace and latitude in your self-evaluation and appreciate this is about making progress and not perfection.[84]

Exercise 3: Finding Your Purpose

I don't want to give the impression that because there are only three steps in my three-step purpose model that this will be easy. Let's give it a try.

Review each question below and reflect upon your answers. If you find that you need to tweak a question because doing so will help you clarify your purpose, feel free to do so. This is your purpose!

1. Describe what you want to be and what you want to do. Think of how you want to feel and what brings you genuine joy, and so on. Think about what you want to be doing. You can be as specific as you want to be in your descriptions.

2. Describe the impact you can have when you are at your best.

3. Why does your purpose matter?

Here's what I came up with by following the three-step purpose model:

1. I want to be happy, healthy, able to work with people I respect and be present for those I love.

2. When I'm at my best, I can love, inspire, help, and enable others to awaken their authenticity and bring their purpose to life.

3. I believe that when people live their purpose authentically, they can pay it forward to others, and the world will be a better place.

Your Purpose

1. Describe what you want to be and what you want to do. Think of how you want to feel and what brings you genuine joy, and so on. Think about what you want to be doing. You can be as specific as you want to be in your descriptions.

2. Describe the impact you can have when you are at your best.

3. Why does your purpose matter?

Reflection

Take a moment now and look at all you've accomplished in this chapter. You've identified the five pivotal moments that have made you "you," you've identified your values, and you've created your purpose. That's amazing. I'm honored to have taken this journey with you!

Can I tell you a secret? I've attended tons of events about values and purpose, and yet I've never managed to work through all these things and get them on paper before. I'm so excited that I have them now!

I created the steps and experienced them, as I hope that you will. I'm happy with the results. I hope that you are as well. As is true with everything else, if you did the work, you would have some significant and helpful information about yourself and what's important to you.

Keeping Your Values and Purpose Alive

I want the work we've just done together to continue to serve you long after you've put this book down. Here are some ways that you can keep your values and purpose alive.

- Post your values and purpose in a place where you'll see them every day.

- Create a vision board (there are some amazing examples online).

- Commit to habits that will bring your purpose to life. Check out the book *Atomic Habits* by James Clear for amazing tips on creating good habits.

- Create a small card that includes them and put it in your wallet.

- Talk about them! I'm known for saying, "One of my personal values is honesty, so please don't ever lie to me."

- Hold yourself accountable for living up to them. If you're at a fork in the road, ask yourself which way is more in line with your values and purpose.

- Think about them as you meditate. If you're not someone who meditates, consider learning about the practice. This is something I personally wish to improve because it's a powerful tool.

- Pray if you believe in doing so.

- Learn about the Law of Attraction. Jen Sincero's *You Are a Badass* and Rhonda Byrne's *The Secret* have good information about the Law of Attraction. This law states that the universe is truly pulling for you, and if you genuinely believe that you can attract the things you want in life, you will.

Key Takeaways

- There are pivotal moments in our lives that represent our life story and greatly influence who we are.

- Values help us understand what's most important to us in life.

- Our purpose evolves, but every human has a purpose. The work of our life is to understand that purpose and use it in a way that helps others.

- Completing the exercises in this chapter will result in your owning and understanding the pivotal moments in your life, your values, and your purpose.

8 YOUR PATH FORWARD

We've done a lot of work together. How are you feeling about your discoveries?

I've taken every step of this journey with you and in doing so I've reawakened my authenticity and reminded myself of my values and purpose. Have you done the same? I truly hope so, but if you're not quite there yet, it's ok. This chapter will build on what you've done so far and help you make some key decisions about your next steps.

Let's quickly revisit what we've learned so far and how it can be used to decide what's next in your journey:

- In Chapter 4 you identified two or three areas where you felt you could be more authentic at work. You also called out your feelings and fears and identified specific improvements that would positively impact your situation.

- Chapter 5 equipped you with tools to help you communicate your needs effectively.

- Chapter 6 addressed conflict, courage, curiosity, and compassion and the role each plays in your authenticity.

- Chapter 7 had exercises that resulted in connecting to pivotal moments in your life, your values, and your purpose.

Now that you've done so much work, what are some ways that you will keep your pivotal moments, values, and purpose top of mind so that you don't lose sight of their importance in your life?

I created a vision board and my purpose statement is front and center on it. Every day when I sit at my computer, I am reminded how I want to treat people, what I want to do and why that's so important. It's a daily reminder of why I'm here. I wish I didn't need a daily reminder for something so important, but the truth is that it's easy to get busy with life and lose sight of our purpose. Please don't let that happen to you.

As I was thinking about this chapter, I took a walk and listened to a podcast with Oprah Winfrey and Alicia Keys as they discussed Key's book *More Myself*. [85] What I learned about Keys is that she's like the rest of us in that she must work hard to stay true to her authentic self. Here are a few pieces of the discussion that I found interesting.

Winfrey: "What you're talking about is the journey that we're all taking. The decisions that we all have to make and that big question of who am I really and how do I stand in the truth of it?"

Keys: "Yeah like how do you know who you are? How do you know? I didn't know who I was, and I still have to constantly remind myself and seek out the truth of who I am right now in this moment. And I don't think there's ever been ah, there's not a person that pushes you mostly in all of our lives to say 'what are you feeling? What are you going through? How do you access yourself?' I mean all we're taught is kind of how to emulate everything else or how to follow the rules or how to do what everyone told us to do so that we can make everybody happy. I mean how do you actually find that way to express and discover what is good for you and to be strong enough to actually claim it?"

Keys has much competition for her time and attention, but she knows she must focus on seeking the truth of who she truly is in this life. When I listened to the podcast, I found it touching that she values knowing and staying in touch with her authentic self.

I obviously don't know her personally, but let me tell you, I cannot listen to her sing without crying! She puts her heart and soul into her music—it gets me every time.

Listen to Your Inner Voice

Before we dive into the work of this chapter, I want to remind you that it's important to listen to yourself. I believe that God (spirit, energy, whatever higher being) nudges us to pay attention in large and small ways. Sometimes the nudges show up as a single thought or feeling that things aren't right. If we make a habit of not listening, the nudges get harder and may even be catastrophic.

You've probably heard people say things like "I heard this little voice telling me I wasn't well" or "I knew I shouldn't marry him, but I couldn't cancel the wedding after paying for the reception!." We get the messages, but we don't always listen.

In Oprah Winfrey's SuperSoul Conversation "Life First Speaks to You in a Whisper," she says:

> You know in all of the years of doing the *Oprah Show,* there were many days that I sat in my chair across from one or two or five or six or seven people and I would be so frustrated because I just wanted to shake people sometimes and say 'why didn't you pay attention to your life?' I said on the show probably – the producers tell me that they counted thirty-three times, but I know I thought it at least a thousand times – I would say listening to your life as it whispers to you first so that it does not have to knock you upside the head with a brick or come crashing down on you as a brick wall is one of the greatest principles of life because there are many things that happen in life that are beyond our control. Natural disasters, death, unexplained events, but there are also many many many things in life which we can control and become out of control because you're just not paying attention. You are sleepwalking through your life and I have seen this so many

times on this show I wanted to take the guests
and go "would you just pay attention!" [86]

What do you think when you read that? Have you been paying attention to life's whispers? I've had times in my life where I was aware that I was losing myself and I heard the whispers. The way this awareness came to me varied depending on how far away from "me" I was getting. Sometimes I'd just feel a little "off," where I knew I wasn't feeling like myself. This would be a "whisper." Once I acknowledged that things weren't quite right, I could get back on track by giving myself a break from my busy schedule and spending time with loved ones.

At other times I was too busy to pay attention and the messages needed to be more painful so I could hear them. I remember a tear-filled time when I was going to night school, working full-time, and had small children. I was in my car alone and feeling overloaded. I remember thinking as tears streamed down my face "I've died, and no one noticed." This is a painful and powerful memory. I was doing far too much, and I didn't know how to ask for help.

That day in the car forced me to see that I was not giving anyone or anything my best self. I was killing myself because I didn't want people thinking that I couldn't keep up with the demands of work, home, and raising our children. I was subconsciously attached to a picture of myself being super-woman and I didn't want anyone thinking that I wasn't able to keep up with the demands that go along with my self-proclaimed designation.

After that sad time in the car, I made some meaningful changes. I stopped ironing all of our clothes (OMG why did I iron baby clothes?), told myself that the house didn't always have to be perfect, and allowed myself to fall short of my own ridiculous expectations.

I was saved by hearing that message in the car that day. I learned so much by understanding the ridiculous demands I was placing on myself. My experience has helped me help others who need to hear that you really can't do everything at once so it's important to pick your priorities carefully.

There was another message from the universe that came to me from someone else. I was feeling drained because my work no longer felt fun, invigorating and purpose driven. I can vividly recall hearing the word "depleted" in my head. Upon hearing it in my head, I nodded in agreement and thought, "that's exactly how I feel!" I wasn't sure what to do about it, but it was an undeniable truth that I acknowledged in that moment.

Later that very same week I went to a company-sponsored wellness event. There was a guest there who was someone who would evaluate your aura and give a reading of your spiritual condition. I wasn't much of a believer in aura reading, but I thought it would be fun to see what she'd say. The woman went through her normal routine with me and ended her time by saying with a somber look on her face "you are depleted." I wanted to cry because I genuinely felt that it was God speaking through her using the exact same word He spoke to me. He wanted me to take notice. Message received!

Reinforcing messages kept coming to me just to be sure I was getting the message. In some ways, I imagine a huddle with all my universal protectors saying, "Geez, this woman is not getting the message—we need to send reinforcements!" I was meeting with an outside consultant and as we were wrapping up our meeting, his face took on a serious expression. He said, "Vicki, I'm worried about you. You're the most effervescent person I know, and it makes me sad to see that you seem to be losing that aspect of yourself." I couldn't argue with him, he was right.

I didn't quit my job or make any dramatic changes right away, but I accepted it as fact that I was losing myself again and that I could and, in fact, I MUST choose a different path forward. I talked to my husband, children, friends, and trusted colleagues. I prayed about it as well. When an opportunity presented itself to me to leave, I was emotionally prepared to do so.

In his book *Spiritual Solutions,* Deepak Chopra explains how the experience I shared happens by saying the following:

> When you can take your awareness outside the place where struggle is ever-present, two things happen at the same time: your awareness expands, and with that, new answers begin to appear. When awareness expands, events that seem random actually aren't. A larger purpose is trying to unfold through you. When you become aware of that purpose—which is unique for each person—you become like an architect who has been handed the blueprint. Instead of laying bricks and fitting pipes at random, the architect can now proceed with confidence that he

knows what the building should look like and how to construct it.[87]

Do these stories resonate with you? Do you feel the nudges from the universe? Are you working to understand them and take action, or do you write them off as just being random thoughts? By the way, the completed exercises in Chapter 7 provide you with the kind of blueprint that Chopra mentions above.

Using Winfrey's analogy, when you pay attention to your feelings, it's much easier to address the pebbles than it is to ignore your feelings and be confronted with a brick wall as a result. The exercises in Chapter 4 provide you with insights into your feelings and fears—that might be a good first step in identifying your pebbles.

Should You Stay or Should You Go?

> *If you quit, please resign.*
> *—Vicki Znavor*

So where do you go from here? Armed with your awareness of the importance of listening to yourself, you have arrived at the fork in the road and there are two paths.

- **Path One**: You stay in your current job, but you commit to bringing more of your authentic self to work.

- **Path Two**: You develop a plan to find a different job that fulfills your purpose.

I didn't give you the option of doing nothing because you wouldn't have made it this far in the book unless you felt compelled to make a change. It's never too late to make a change. With that in mind, let's dig deeper on both options.

Reasons to Stay Where You Are

Sometimes we get irritated with our work situations and our first thought is to leave and start over somewhere else. I've always counseled people who are thinking about leaving their jobs to think about why they're leaving and to assess if there are reasons to stay.

Beverly Kaye and Sharon Jordan-Evans surveyed more than 17,000 employees with various organizations for their book *Love 'Em or Lose 'Em* about why people stay with an organization.[88] Here are the top 10 reasons from their survey:

1. Exciting work and challenge
2. Career growth, learning, and development
3. Working with great people
4. Fair pay
5. Supportive management/good boss
6. Being recognized, valued, and respected
7. Benefits
8. Meaningful work and making a difference
9. Pride in the organization, its mission, and its products
10. Great work environment and culture

Let's dig deeper into each of the reasons to stay listed above.

Exercise 1

This exercise is designed to help you take inventory of the positive aspects of your current situation and to improve aspects that aren't as positive as you'd like them to be. Let's walk through the exercise.

Step 1: Read each reason to stay. If you feel that the reason to stay applies in your current work situation, make note of it. Sometimes seeing positive aspects of your work situation on paper gives you a healthy perspective and an appreciation for what you already have.

Step 2: Next, look at the Steps to Take. These are suggestions for things you can do to improve your work situation.

Ok, let's get started.

Reasons to Stay

My work is exciting and challenging.

This is great! Think about what work you enjoy most. If it helps, write it down.

Steps to Take

- Make note of what you like most about your work because this helps you know with certainty what you wish to continue doing no matter where you work.

- If your work isn't exciting, research other jobs (internal and external) that incorporate the aspects of your work that you enjoy most. Knowing what you love to do is a fundamental step in building a rewarding career.

I have opportunities to grow my career, learn new things, and develop professionally.

If you have this in your current work situation, it's a blessing. Keep learning and growing by taking on additional assignments, attending conferences or taking courses.

Steps to Take

- If you don't have an opportunity to grow and develop, identify an experience or course that you know will benefit you and the company.

- Talk to your manager, explain the benefits, and ask if you can get the experience you'd like or take the course. It never hurts to ask so don't hesitate to do so. If your manager says that the company isn't willing to pay the cost, ask your manager for his/her support in gaining the experience you need. If you have no other choice, consider if this learning is important enough for you to pay for it yourself.

I really like and respect the people I work with.

Working with people you like and respect is a good way to spend your time at work. Let them know that you appreciate them.

Steps to Take

- If you feel no one is great to work with in your present workplace, consider if you're failing to see the good in others.

I am paid well for the work that I do.

Steps to Take

- If you're not paid well for the work that you do, look at similar jobs and know specifically what you should be paid. With an understanding of the right level of compensation, share your findings with your manager and ask them what it would take for you to be paid appropriately for the job you're doing.

My manager is supportive and cares about me.

Having a supportive manager is one of the most important aspects of work. What do you like most about your manager? Consider ways that you can start building the same skills that you admire in your manager. This is a great way to prepare for being a good manager in the future.

Steps to Take

- If you don't feel your manager is supportive, be sure that you are reading your manager's attitude toward you properly. It's appropriate to ask your manager if you have their support if you're uncertain. If your manager truly does not support you, understand why that's the case and start preparing to move on. It is nearly impossible to succeed without your manager's support.

My work is valued, and I feel appropriately recognized and respected.

If you feel valued, recognized and respected, feel good about it.

Steps to Take

- If you feel your work isn't valued, it's important to understand what's going on. Read your performance appraisal and reflect upon conversations with your manager. Has your manager given you feedback that you aren't willing to accept? Leo's story in Chapter 3 may be helpful to reread.

- Ask your manager what you can do to be valued and respected going forward.

   My benefits package meets my needs and is affordable.

Benefits are an important part of your total rewards that should be appreciated.

Steps to Take

- If your benefits package doesn't meet your needs, do the following:
  - Call your benefits representative to make sure you understand the company's offerings. It's not

uncommon for employees to misunderstand what's available to them. Talk to the people who know these plans inside and out.

- Do your homework and identify your specific needs and talk to your manager. Sometimes management loses sight of employee needs so your feedback may be helpful to the company and other employees.

The work I do is meaningful to myself and others and I feel I am making a difference.

This is an important and fulfilling aspect of work.

Steps to Take

- Are you certain there are no aspects of your work that are meaningful? If so, consider what you can do to change this. Can you help your company's employee resource councils or participate in volunteer efforts?

- Speak with your manager and ask them how your work supports the company's success. Tell your manager that this is an important aspect of your work.

- Ask your manager how they find personal meaning in their work.

I'm proud of the organization where I work, its mission and its products and services.

Steps to Take

- What would make you prouder? Can you make some suggestions to your manager or others at your company?

My work environment and culture are great.

Steps to Take

- What would a great culture/work environment look like for you? Use this insight to evaluate other companies to work for.

Other reasons to stay

- Make note of any good reasons to stay.

Having a Job is a Good Reason to Stay

The economy in 2020 is more volatile than I've ever seen in my career. It makes sense to appreciate having a job and being cautious about making a change when so much is uncertain.

My advice to anyone who isn't in an ideal situation but doesn't want to risk being unemployed is to not let this stop you from taking some proactive steps now.

The Steps to Take on the previous pages provide you with some specific actions you can take now to improve your situation. Another step you can take now is to strengthen your financial position and ultimately prepare for a change when it makes sense for you to do so.

Does your company have an employee assistance program (EAP)? This is a consistently underutilized benefit at many companies. Did you know that many EAPs offer at least a few free counseling sessions with a financial planner? Often your 401k program and open enrollment sessions provide immensely helpful information to employees. Become a well-informed consumer of your company's offerings!

Did anything surprise you from this exercise? Are the positives that you've identified good enough for you to stay? Everyone's life situation is different. Only you can know whether it makes sense for you to stay in your position or to leave.

Make note of the steps to take that you're willing to commit to taking and commit to completing them in a reasonable amount of time.

Reasons to Leave

> *Work shouldn't suck the soul out of your body.*
> *—Vicki Znavor*

Chapters 5 and 6 include several examples of difficult work situations. Do any of them apply to you? The exercises, when completed, help you identify ways to improve those situations. Rereading the relevant chapters and your completed exercises will be helpful in deciding if you've done all you can to improve things at work.

Sometimes leaving is clearly the best move for you, especially if you receive an offer for a job that better aligns with your purpose, values, and pays you well. Go for it!

Sometimes leaving feels right because you are tired of being passed up for great opportunities and/or appropriate compensation. I understand this rationale well. In the article "12 People Share Why They Quit Their Jobs," I noticed one story that most of us can relate to at one time or another in our careers.

It was the second time that I asked for a small raise, and they said there was nothing they could do for me—despite the fact we had new expensive furniture from Crate & Barrel ordered to the office every couple of days.

It was crushing to hear because I had waited half a year to ask again, and during that time, I started doing three times the work and took on tasks like coding, design, and event logistics on top of my marketing job. People would always praise me on what a valuable asset I was, but it just didn't add up by the way they compensated me. I knew I had to go when it felt like a new couch was worth more than the value I was bringing to the company.[89]

If, despite identifying and suggesting the changes you believed would help in Chapters 4 and 5, your health or general well-being are being negatively impacted, consider leaving. "High levels of stress actually cause real physical symptoms, which is not something you should be feeling towards your job."[90]

In the article "When Burnout Is a Sign You Should Leave Your Job," Monique Valcour describes burnout well:

A sustainable job leverages your strengths and helps you perform at your peak. One of the most consistently demoralizing experiences my coaching clients report is having to work in conditions that constrain their performance to a level well below their potential – for example, overwhelming workload, conflicting objectives, unclear expectations, inadequate resources, and a lack of managerial support. Persistent barriers to good performance thwart the human need for mastery.

She goes on to say, "Burnout is like a relationship that's gone bad: When the employment relationship is no longer beneficial to either party, and the prospects for reviving it are dim, it may be time to call it quits."[91]

Work shouldn't suck your soul out of your body. If the above describes your situation, ask yourself why this is even minimally acceptable to you. You deserve better and you can get it if you make the effort to do so.

Another good reason to consider leaving is if your company isn't doing well financially. Read what others are saying about your company and pay attention to internal or external commentary about reducing expenses or possible layoffs.

You don't have to leave immediately, but you should develop a plan to do so. I've provided you with several actions to consider. Select some and/or create additional actions and then go about completing them. Be sure to identify the kind of work you want to do that supports your purpose, the minimum salary you will need to earn and the kind of values that your future company must have in place. Spend quality time researching companies to find the best place for "you."

Speaking of layoffs, sometimes you will be asked to leave for no other reason than the company must reduce expenses. This is a difficult situation to be in, but I want you to know that everyone I've ever known who has experienced this has gone on to better opportunities after being laid off. The perfect job doesn't always come about quickly, but it happens. Hang in there. Take advantage of everything you're offered by your employer such as outplacement counseling. Ask your HR department to explain anything that's not clear in your exit package as well. Let HR and anyone else that offers to help you do so.

Leaving with Grace

Leaving a job is difficult, no matter what. It is more difficult if you have resentment due to the nature of your departure. Been there. It's human nature to want to talk negatively about anyone who disappointed you in some way.

My mother-in-law used to use the expression "never spit in a well, you may have to come back for a drink" and it seems like good advice here, albeit perhaps a bit dated. In the heat of the moment, it might feel good to tell others that your boss was an incompetent jerk or that your company was horrible. Unfortunately, by sharing this kind of information, you may be giving the impression that you're unprofessional to people who can help you at a future point in your career. Newton's Third Law of Motion discussed in Chapter 6 applies here as well.

In the article "Should You Stay at Your Current Job," Shelcy Joseph gives great advice:

> No matter the circumstances that brought you to pursuing the next step in your career, be sure to leave your job in a professional way by giving proper notice, respecting relationships and offering yourself as a resource. It's a small world and you never know

when your boss or colleagues might turn up as a customer or client in the future.[92]

It's also important to not disparage the company or your colleagues on social media. If you have constructive advice that can be shared on sites like Glassdoor, provide it in a professional manner.

In the article "How to Quit a Job You Hate with Grace," Thomas Heath points out that "if you would like to have a good life and land well, take revenge out of the equation."[93]

I found this quote that summed up the concept of revenge so well:

> *Before you embark on a journey of revenge, dig two graves.*[94]
> — *Confucius*

Pick Your Confidants Well

We all need someone to share our feelings with as we make our way through the highs and lows of life. Pick your confidants carefully. They should be people you know you can trust and who have your best interests in mind. They also should be people who will challenge your assumptions, not "yes" people.

Expect Grief

Change of any kind is a loss. Losses usually result in grief, even if your change will lead you to something spectacular.

Once when I was preparing to leave the company that I had been at for most of my career, I worried that this change would seriously impact my mental state. After all, I loved the people there so much that I anticipated feeling deep grief and I was scared that it might be more than I could handle. I decided to see a therapist *before* I left the company because I wanted my last day to feel as though it was simply ending a nice chapter in my life and nothing more.

I was able to talk with my therapist about my sense of loss and I am so glad that I did. Another unexpected benefit was that I found myself again.

I remember that last day so well. I had cleaned out my office in advance except for, of all things, my desk lamp. I remember walking down the hall, lamp in hand thinking, "I'm leaving and I'm taking my light with me!" I did indeed. Every work experience afterward was deeper and more meaningful in my career, but I needed this experience to fully appreciate those in the future.

Everyone's feelings are different, but I want to suggest to you that if you feel you need some extra support as you prepare to leave your job, please get it. Don't forget that most employee assistance programs (EAP) offer at least a few therapy sessions for free, so this is a great way to use the benefit and get the help you need for free.

In some ways, it's healthy to always be prepared to leave an organization. Save your money, keep refining and growing your skills, keep up with your networking activities, and always know your worth. It's empowering when you know you can leave if you want to do so.

Key Takeaways

- God or if you prefer the universe, nudges you towards your life's purpose. Listen to your inner voice for guidance.

- It's helpful to understand whether you should stay in or leave your current job. Complete the exercises in this chapter to understand your best path forward.

- Always leave a position or company with grace; it will serve you well.

- Don't forget to get free assistance from your company's EAP if you have this benefit.

9 LETTING GO

I decided to call this chapter "Letting Go" because we can't live up to our purpose without letting go of the things that get in the way. Often these "things" are our own limiting beliefs about who we are and what we're capable of doing.

Listen to the Whispers

This morning as I sat down at my computer to begin this chapter, I cried - I haven't done that in a long time and it felt good. As the tears streamed down my face, I reflected on how much my life has changed in such a short time. I miss working with the people I worked with previously because they were friends. If I think about it too much, I feel a profound loss. I know that 2020 was a weird year and in some ways we've all experienced loss in one form or another.

There were a lot of great changes as well. I moved to a house that feels right, wrote a book with my dog sitting next to me, found a renewed sense of purpose and I have dinner every night with my husband. None of these things would've happened had the changes in 2020 not occurred.

Remember what we learned in Chapter 8: life first speaks to us in whispers? If we fail to listen to the whispers, they get louder and even painful until we pay attention. When we pay attention, our authenticity is reawakened, and we are reminded of our purpose. It happens over and over in our lives.

Today I was looking for a book. I didn't find the book I wanted, but I found the one I needed: *A Year of Living Mindfully* by Anna Black.[95] I flipped through the book and found a long-forgotten exercise that I'd completed. Here's what I wrote:

> I'm not paying attention to the people or things that matter most to me. I'm not productive. I feel that my mindset isn't helpful to me. I'm worried about how I'm spending my time and I worry that I'll look back at this time and regret how I'm spending it. I'm never 100% present! That's not how I want to spend my life.

Seeing the words I wrote that day makes me sad. While I'm in a great place now, some of the changes I experienced in 2020 were *painful*. I heard the whispers from the universe for some time and even wrote them as you see above, but I kept putting my purpose aside. I was essentially saying to God and the angels that I know surround me "I know that the way I'm spending my time these days isn't aligned with my purpose, but I'll get back to that as soon as I can." I don't know how God felt about my promise, but I do know my life is dramatically different now—in a good way.

I've let go of what I thought this year would be as well as what I thought I would do for the rest of my career. Now I'm open to the possibilities and I have a hunch they're better than what I can imagine.

Are you listening to your whispers? Think about that for a moment. If it helps, go stand in front of a mirror, look yourself in the eyes and think about what the universe is saying to you.

Your Past Is Not Your Future

> *You can't make room for your future self if you keep dragging your past with you.*
>
> —*Vicki Znavor*

In Chapter 7, you identified your life's pivotal moments. Take some time to reflect on them. Honor and be grateful for those moments because they made you "you" but make a conscientious effort to put them away. If it helps, think of your past as being a photo album that you've put away and take out only when you're feeling nostalgic. It holds special memories for you, but you don't take it to work with you every day.

I know a wonderful young woman. She's brilliant, funny, kind, caring and lovely in every way. Seriously, she's a rock star. Years ago, while still a teen, she felt she disappointed her family. She has carried guilt unnecessarily for many years and it's impacted how she feels about herself. Her family couldn't be any prouder of her if they tried and yet she feels such a burden.

I was speaking with her recently and I asked her if this is a weight that she wishes to continue carrying for the rest of her life. I wanted her to consider how carrying this burden is serving her life. She gets to decide if this is what she wants, but who would want to do that?

I have friends and family who made mistakes while they were young (and don't we all?). As a result, they seem to think that those past mistakes define their decision-making abilities for life. Why?

I've also known people who have held high-powered jobs and sacrificed everything to succeed. Once they leave their jobs, they struggle finding their place in the world, a place that's no longer attached to a title or a company.

There are other aspects of our past that we cling to that don't serve us well. Maybe we weren't great at something (athletics, school, relationships, certain jobs, finances, decision-making, etc. before. Does it mean that we'll never be good at those things? Of course not!

Letting go of your past while still honoring and respecting it is a healthy path forward. If you've made mistakes or have regrets, consider what you've learned from them, but don't drag them into your future.

I've added an exercise so that you can make note of the aspects of your life that you're not willing to take into your future.

Exercise

Think about the beliefs that aren't serving you and decide how you'll address/resolve them. I've included a sample matrix below to help you.

Beliefs Not Serving Me Well	A Path Forward
I've disappointed people I care about	• Talk to them! • Consider if this disappointment is simply a story you've told yourself • Apologize if appropriate
I messed up at work and now I'll never get promoted	• Make every effort to understand what you did wrong • What did you learn from your mistake? • Talk to your manager, describe what you did wrong and what you've learned. • Ask your manager what it'll take to get back on track. • See Chapter 5 for more tips.

Complete the matrix below with any beliefs not serving you well.

Beliefs Not Serving Me Well	A Path Forward

Take some time to take in the impact of the beliefs not serving you well. How are they preventing you from moving forward in the way that you'd like? Are you committed to a path forward?

Your Values Are Your North Star

My personal values are my North Star. You listed your values in Chapter 7. When you're faced with a decision—doesn't matter if it's personal or professional—your values will guide you to the path that works best for you.

Some people are a little wishy-washy on values. If you're wishy-washy about what you've listed as your values, they are not your deeply held values. Revisit the work you did on your values in Chapter 7. You'll know they're right when you feel emotional about the list you create.

Here's how I feel about my values: I won't back down on them. If you ask me to do something or behave in a way that is against my values, I will dig in my heels and not budge from my position. It's non-negotiable. Your values should create a similar feeling for you.

When you're clear on your values, you're clear about so many things in life. In some ways it's a little like wearing glasses. Blurred lines suddenly go away when seen through the lens of values.

Decide what your values mean to you and the extent to which you're willing to accommodate situations that violate them. It's not always possible to adhere to your values perfectly, but if something bumps up against them, it should be readily apparent to you because you'll feel uncomfortable. When that happens, stop, and carefully consider your next steps.

If you're stuck with a decision at work, talk to your manager about why going one way or another is either in or out of alignment with your personal values. This kind of discussion is respected by leaders who also have strong values.

One tool that I've used in my life is asking myself if doing something could result in a deathbed regret. In other words, if I do something now that I know is against my values, how will that feel when I'm dying? Or how would I feel if my kids found out that I did something against my values? Let me tell you, thinking about things in this way has prevented me from doing things I knew I'd regret.

No one is perfect. We all make mistakes. One way to avoid a deathbed regret is that if you know you screwed up, make it right. It doesn't matter if your regret happened years ago, if you're still thinking about it then make it right. Don't let your pride get in the way. Apologize and mean it, learn from it, make it right and move on.

Just yesterday, I received a heartwarming and unexpected note from someone. Facebook disagreements can be so silly sometimes. She disagreed with me quite harshly on the presidential election in 2016. She sent me a private note indicating that she was out of line and genuinely sorry for her behavior.

I was so touched by her note; it took guts to write it. I responded with the gratitude and love that she deserved. I know for sure that we both felt a weight lift from our shoulders.

Let go of behavior and relationships that aren't in alignment with your values and absolutely let go of any belief that it's too late to make things right without any expectations from whomever you've hurt. They may not respond the way you hope they will and that's ok. You've done the right thing by apologizing and it'll feel good.

Face Your Fears

Every human being on this planet is afraid of something. You can own your fear, or it can own you. We covered fear in Chapters 4 and 5 using the F3 model, which helps you understand your feelings, fears, and a way forward. Admittedly it's difficult to cover all the ways that fear can impact one's life, but I covered several workplace fears.

Often fears at work are made up in our minds. For example, I know a young woman who believes that if she misses a day of work, she'll be fired. She's a great employee so her fear isn't logical.

Sometimes the very people you're intimidated by or fearful of at work act in a domineering way because they're fearful and/or insecure themselves. If you see someone—even a senior person—acting in an overly domineering or assertive way, just think to yourself, "Ah, you're insecure!" Keep it to yourself and know that confident people don't go out of their way to dominate others. Knowing this empowers you to not fear them, but instead to feel badly for them. This shift in thinking is helpful in managing your fear.

Let go of the power you're giving to fear. This reminds me of the following story:

> One evening an old Cherokee told his grandson about a battle that goes on inside people.
>
> He said, "My son, the battle is between two 'wolves' inside us all.

One is evil. It is anger, envy, jealousy, sorrow, regret, greed, arrogance, self-pity, guilt, resentment, inferiority, lies, false pride, superiority and ego.

The other is good. It is joy, peace, love, hope, serenity, humility, kindness, benevolence, empathy, generosity, truth, compassion and faith.

The grandson thought about it for a minute and then asked his grandfather: 'Which wolf wins?"

The old Cherokee simply replied, "The one you feed."[96]

Before I close out this section, trust your instincts if you fear that someone could harm you or others. Contact HR immediately. Don't wait until tomorrow—do it now. Whenever workplace violence occurs, someone inevitably shares after the fact that there were clues that this could occur. Don't be that person.

Watch Your Ego

When Wayne Dyer was asked to explain the concept of "ego," he said:

All it is, it's an idea that we carry around. You know what the idea of the ego is? It says: "I am what I have, I am what I do, I am what other people think of me. I'm separate from everybody else, I'm separate from what's missing in my life, and I'm separate from God." [97]

Deepak Chopra talks about ego this way:

> The ego, however, is not who you really are. The ego is your self-image; it is your social mask; it is the role you are playing. Your social mask thrives on approval. It wants to control, and it is sustained by power, because it lives in fear.
>
> Your true Self, which is your spirit, your soul, is completely free of those things. It is immune to criticism, it is unfearful of any challenge, and it feels beneath no one. And yet, it is also humble and feels superior to no one, because it recognizes that everyone else is the same Self, the same spirit in different disguises.[98]

When you move up the corporate ladder, you are rewarded with pay and prestige and people treat you differently. Some people will agree to things you say, just because of the position you hold. They will laugh at your jokes even when they're not funny and they'll use your name when sharing stories at corporate events because they want to stroke your ego. If you're not careful, you'll start to believe the hype about yourself.

It's easy to lose your true self by believing that you are what you do, what you have and what people think of you. Being authentic requires that you know yourself and your values throughout your life despite all the fakery that comes at you.

Be proud of your work and your contributions. If you get a great raise and a promotion—that's cause for celebration. Just don't lose sight of who you are in the process. You are not what you do. If you lose your job, you're still you. You are not what you have. If all your possessions are taken away, you're still you. And you are not what people think about you, whether those thoughts are good or bad.

There are some outstanding books by Dyer, Chopra, and Eckhart Tolle that talk about ego far more eloquently that I can. We are all so much more than what we do and as we live our purpose, this becomes increasingly more obvious.

Be a Light to Others

Every human being on this planet is struggling in some way. If you choose to do so, you can be a light for others as they proceed through this life. You don't have to like everyone, but if you can find ways to help and support others it will enhance your life's purpose.

If someone aggravates you as you're engaging with them, take a moment to think to yourself "I honor this person's journey in life. Let me be a light in whatever way possible to this person in this moment." Now, I'm not suggesting that you allow them to treat you badly, but sometimes just interrupting negative energy with positive energy changes the dynamic of a conversation.

I was speaking with a former colleague on this topic. She shared that a senior leader that she supports has been rude to her lately and hasn't shared information that she needs to do her job. To further complicate the situation, her manager told her not to communicate with the executive directly. So, the executive gets to be rude to her, but she doesn't get to respond because she's too far down the chain of command. Her situation seems ridiculous and unfair, but this stuff happens in the corporate world all the time. Because they haven't talked, the negativity has lingered unnecessarily for two months.

My former colleague is an incredibly positive person who cares about the company and this executive. They've had a good working relationship until recently and, if "allowed" to do so, she could change this dynamic.

The Intentional Compassionate Conflict Model shared in Chapter 6 is a great way to prepare for the conversation. My advice to her was to use the model to determine what she would say to the executive and then she should share that with her manager and specifically request that she be "allowed" to talk to the executive. I know that her approach would be to say that things had changed between them and she'd like to understand what's happened so she can work with him to make it right.

Knowing the executive, I think he'd be sorry that he acted so poorly and would apologize. But even if he didn't, she could feel good about how she behaved.

Let go of any belief that your age or level in an organization prevents you from being a light to someone else – even someone else who is more senior to you. Everyone, no matter their position in the hierarchy can use a ray of light sometimes.

Find Gratitude

> *Gratitude is a powerful catalyst for happiness. It's the spark that lights a fire of joy in your soul.*[99]
>
> — *Amy Collette*

Finding something every day for which you are grateful will add perspective and joy to your life. What are you grateful for today? If you're struggling to find anything, here are a few things to consider:

- Do you have a roof over your head?
- Do you know where your next meal is coming from?
- Are you healthy?
- Do you have some good friends?

If you have these basic things, you are one of the most fortunate humans on the planet! Be grateful for them – they're not guaranteed to anyone.

If you're not where you want to be in your career, that's OK. Be grateful for your journey; it's the only one like it that's ever existed. It helps to shift your inner dialogue. Instead of saying "Ugh, I have to go to work today," say "I get to go to work today and I'm going to be spectacular!" Or you can say to yourself "I'm not yet where I want to be, but I'm on my way to something better!"

I used to work with a wonderful woman named Kristin. While in her forties she learned she had breast cancer. One day I ran into her and she said "you know what? I'd give anything to have another shitty day at the office." Sadly, she lost her battle with cancer, but the memory of that conversation and its impact on me will stay with me forever.

We take so much for granted, even crappy days at work. Compared to cancer, even the worst day at work deserves our gratitude.

Let go of feeling that you have nothing for which to be grateful. You do. And know that you can be someone that others are grateful to have in their lives as well.

You Are Good Enough

My goodness, please know that you are good enough to do all that you genuinely want to do. Think about all you've experienced so far and know that the only person that can get in your way is you. You don't have to spend any energy convincing someone else that you're good enough, you just have to convince yourself.

There's a scene in the movie *The Holiday* that I love. Kate Winslet as Iris is having dinner with Eli Wallach who plays Arthur. Iris is in tears as she describes her disappointing love life. Arthur says this to her:

> Iris, in the movies they have leading ladies and they have the best friend. You, I can tell are the leading lady, but for some reason you are behaving as the best friend." Iris responds with "you're so right. You're supposed to be the leading lady of your own life for God's sake!"[100]

Let go of any notion or excuse you've been holding on to that you cannot be the leading lady (or man!) of your own life.

Get Going

You know what it means to be authentic. You know your pivotal life stories, your values and your purpose and you've placed them in a place that you will see every day. You understand what you're afraid of and have identified ways to overcome your fear. You know how to resolve conflict with compassion. And you know that life is too short to spend it as someone else.

So, here's one last exercise.

Exercise: Create Your Action Plan

What I Will Do	Why I Must Do It	Start Date	Finish Date

Look back at Chapter 4 to see if there are actions that you identified to help you overcome your fear.

Here's what Paula's scenario looked like in Chapters 4 and 5. Overcoming her fear is critically important for her well-being. She learned that she could overcome her fear by taking the actions listed in the right-hand column.

Feelings	What Will Make It Better? (What Will I Do?)	What Am I Afraid of?	How Can I Overcome My Fear? (What Will I Do?)
I dread going to work because I have too much to do and I don't feel I'll ever catch up.	I need to give my boss some specific examples of why I feel this way and I need their help to make work more manageable.	I'm afraid they'll think I'm incompetent and will fire me.	I will provide specific examples of my workload and ask them to help me prioritize. I will provide suggestions for solving the problem. I will apply their suggestions and keep them regularly updated on how things are going.

I'm taking the right-hand column from Paula's grid and have added the tasks with timelines. I've added one last step at the bottom and that is to assess if the steps are working as hoped. If not, she needs to determine what else she should do.

What I Will Do	Why I Must Do It	Start Date	Finish Date
I will provide specific examples of my workload and ask them to help me prioritize.	I cannot meet all the demands placed on me.		
I will provide suggestions for solving the problem.	This will help my manager as well as demonstrate that I have considered solutions.		
I will apply their suggestions and keep them regularly updated on how things are going.	This shows that I am taking my manager's advice.		
I will schedule time with my manager to provide regular updates	This builds a stronger relationship between us and we'll have a shared understanding of the issues		
Are these steps helping? If not, what else should be done?			

Maybe your tasks will focus on resolving conflict. In Chapter 6 you learned the Intentional Compassionate Conflict Model. If you identified a conflict, make resolving it one of your tasks.

If you want to do something new at work, your tasks can be identifying what you want to do, what skills you need to do it, gaining the skills and then applying for the position.

If you want to build or improve relationships, identify what you will do and hold yourself accountable.

If you want to follow more of your passions, plan your next steps and DO THEM.

My husband used to have a typing teacher back in the 1970s. While he was teaching, he would give advice to his students. He'd be happy to know that this one has stuck with my husband nearly forty years after he sat in his classroom: "The journey of a thousand miles starts with one step."

You don't have to turn your world upside down in a week or even at all. But take action. This is your life.

I found much inspiration from David Viscott's work, so it seems appropriate to add more of his wisdom:

Don't Be Afraid of Your Dream

Your dream is the infancy of your gift. Your belief in your dream makes it a reality. Abandon yourself to your dream. Let go. Dream the dream that has been within you forever. Be the child in your dreams. Value closeness. Play with light. Lose yourself in your senses, and see the world anew. Be the hero in your dreams. Save the nations. Bridge the flood. Conquer evil. Build the peace. The world needs your dreams. Carry them forward. Claim and deliver them. You find yourself by living your dream.[101]

10   100 WAYS TO AUTHENTICITY

1. Think of at least one thing to be grateful for before you get out of bed.

2. Remind yourself of your values.

3. Remind yourself of your purpose.

4. Determine 1-3 top priorities for the day and get them done.

5. Think about 1 thing that you're proud of yourself for at least once a week

6. Work out.

7. Take a walk.

8. Take a nice shower or hot bath.

9. Moisturize.

10. Wear clothes that make you feel great.

11. Get at least 7 hours of sleep.

12. Say "no" when you want to say no.

13. Reach out to at least one person that you care about.

14. Tell your family you love them.

15. Prepare to contribute at meetings.

16. Let someone know if their expectations are unrealistic.

17. Say you're sorry, but only if you mean it.

18. Show appreciation to others as often as possible.

19. Schedule time to handle emails.

20. Ask for help.

21. Avoid watching too much news.

22. If someone interrupts you, say "excuse me, I wasn't finished."

23. If someone is rude to you, tell them that their behavior isn't acceptable.

24. If you miss someone, tell them.

25. Eat as healthy as possible.

26. Drink water.

27. Laugh at least once every day.

28. Read a book.

29. Eliminate anything that feels like a waste of time.

30. Identify something that will save time at work and share it with your manager.

31. If you've hurt someone, apologize.

32. Limit the time you spend scrolling social media.

33. Journal.

34. Do one thing you love at least once a week.

35. Identify anything that makes you angry and then understand why.

36. Pick one thing you've been putting off and make a plan for getting it done.

37. Make a point of noticing one beautiful thing in nature per week.

38. Look at your co-workers and think of them as human beings.

39. Volunteer.

40. Read about the ego.

41. Pick one thing that you do that's ego driven and decide what you'll do about it.

42. Get your medical checkups.

43. Ask someone if they need help and really mean it.

44. Eat even the simplest of dinners at your table instead of the couch.

45. Think of one thing you appreciate about your boss and then tell him/her.

46. Let someone "win" a disagreement.

47. Celebrate the good things in your life.

48. Don't gossip.

49. Don't tell people's secrets.

50. Spend your money wisely.

51. Learn something new every month.

52. If you make a mistake, apologize, learn from it, and move on.

53. Identify the most productive time in your day and plan your work accordingly.

54. Stop spending time with people who you don't enjoy being with.

55. Look people directly in the eye when speaking with them.

56. Talk to someone who has a role that you aspire to have one day and ask him/her what you need to do to do the work they do.

57. Meet one new person at work every month.

58. Look at your LinkedIn profile: does it represent you well?

59. Encourage others to participate in meetings or other work events.

60. Don't allow yourself to think you're lesser than anyone.

61. Don't allow yourself to think you're better than anyone.

62. Don't put something in an email that you wouldn't say to their face directly.

63. Don't say something behind someone's back that you wouldn't say to their face.

64. Don't allow someone to speak for you – speak for yourself.

65. Get a mentor. Read the book *One Minute Mentoring* and prepare for mentoring discussions.

66. Mentor someone else.

67. Don't speak negatively about your manager.

68. Report harassment of any kind to HR.

69. Don't get involved romantically with co-workers.

70. Don't drink at company events.

71. Dress professionally at work and all work events.

72. Pay your bills.

73. Don't date married people.

74. Don't break your vows.

75. Engage in healthy conflict.

76. Check the accuracy of your work.

77. If someone takes credit for your work, speak with your manager.

78. Don't take credit for someone else's work.

79. If you don't know an answer, say you don't know but you'll find out the answer.

80. Do something that scares you once in a while.

81. If you want to take on an assignment at work, tell your manager; don't wait for someone to ask you.

82. Tell the truth in interviews.

83. Don't express anger at work without planning your words.

84. Know that you don't have to be perfect.

85. Believe that you deserve good things in life and work.

86. If an assignment is taking longer than you planned, let your manager know as soon as possible.

87. Help others at work succeed without expecting anything in return.

88. If you're happy, show it.

89. Don't accept a job that you know you don't want.

90. Be genuinely happy for others when they're happy.

91. Compete with your best self, not with anyone else.

92. Don't beat yourself up for mistakes.

93. Don't downplay your abilities.

94. Encourage others to do their best.

95. Decorate your home with things you genuinely love.

96. Live within your means.

97. Accept that you are in charge of your life.

98. Share only what you wish about yourself.

99. Tell your loved ones the things they need to know but do it with love.

100. Never give up on your dreams.

Before You Go

We've been on quite a journey together haven't we? I hope this book has helped you find your authenticity and that you're determined to keep it alive throughout your life. You are here for a reason, my friend. Don't ever let lose sight of this important fact.

As I look back on my forty years of work, I wish that I would've learned some of the lessons I've shared with you much earlier in my career. You're already well ahead of me in your journey. I didn't appreciate the power of authenticity until much later in my life.

What I know now that I didn't know earlier is that you can't control all of the things that happen to you, but you can control how you show up to handle them. I also know that people aren't perfect so expecting perfection of yourself and others is a big waste of time.

Every person that you encounter is doing their best to find their way in this life. Sometimes we desperately want others to see us, but there's such strength in knowing ourselves and then seeing the humanity in others.

The next time you're at work, look around and see your colleagues as human beings who have come to work with their own unique life stories. Some are dealing with things that'll break your heart. No one's life is perfect. Truly see them.

My hope for you is that you find great joy in this life and that you give it to others with wild abandon. Allow yourself to love others with all your heart. Show that you care about others every chance you get and know that there are endless opportunities to do this at work.

Being with you in this way has been such an honor. I had no idea what this experience would be, but I've loved writing with you in mind. I don't know what the next step in my journey is, but this one has forever changed me. I hope it's changed you as well.

The original title of this book was going to be *Life Is Too Short to Spend with Assholes*. While I changed the title for a variety of reasons, I think the sentiment is spot on. You have things to do in this life and you deserve all the joy that comes your way. Spend your time with people who you love and who love you right back.

Be your best, beautiful, authentic self in this life. You're here for a reason. I invite you to visit my website, www.vick-iznavor.com. I'm excited to spend more time with you!

With much love and a big hug,
Vicki

ACKNOWLEDGMENTS

How does one adequately express the deepest gratitude possible in a few typed words? It's not possible, but I'll do my best.

First, I'd like to thank my husband Tom. You've given me the space I need to chase my dreams even when doing so meant you had to change your schedule or do more than your fair share at home which happened a lot. You're the most amazing father to our girls, a wonderful grandfather, and my favorite man on the planet. I love you!

Jennifer, thank you for teaching me how to be a mom. I'm so proud of you for so many reasons. You're a wonderful wife, mother and nurse who gives so much of yourself to others. I also appreciate the time you spent helping me with this book! I've learned so much by being your mom. Thank you and always know that I love you!

Elizabeth, you're an amazing wife, mother, and marketing pro. Your help with this book has been tremendous and I really couldn't have done this without you. It's been fun watching you do what you do so well. I'm so proud of you. I've learned so much by being your mom. Thank you and always know that I love you!

Stephanie, you're a wonderful wife and nurse. I'm so proud of all that you do to help others. You have always been such a great sport, attending countless band concerts and dance recitals basically since you were born. You will always be our baby girl. I've learned so much by being your mom. Thank you and always know that I love you!

To our sweet grandchildren: Bill, Lily, Jack, and Bryan. I love you so much.

Buster, I know you can't read, but I loved writing with you napping next to my desk. You and I have had a great summer and I appreciate how you listened to me reading aloud as I worked through this book. You are the best dog in the world and I love you.

Thanks to the rest of my family – I love you all!

To the late Mary Hanis and Jane DePeugh. You were the teachers who saw potential in me and encouraged me to do well in school. The joy you found in teaching was inspirational. Your students, especially this one, learned so much from you. Thank you so very much.

Thank you to anyone with whom I've ever worked. I've learned so much from you and wish you only the absolute best in life.

Many thanks and much gratitude to my amazing publisher, Melissa Wilson at Networlding Publishing. Melissa, you coached and guided me throughout this process and I'm forever grateful. I loved working with and learning from you. Thank you from the bottom of my heart.

And thanks to you, the reader. I hope that this is just the start of a wonderful relationship. I thought of you with every word in this book. Please visit me at www.vickiznavor.com.

I hope that you've enjoyed reading this book. Please leave a review on Amazon.com.

With love,
Vicki

ABOUT THE AUTHOR

Vicki Znavor learned a long time ago that the only way to be fulfilled in life and at work is to be yourself. After spending four decades helping countless people succeed at work, she is taking another step in living her purpose by writing this book. She knows that great work is done by people who show up as themselves and do work that they genuinely love doing.

Vicki has been recognized by Crain's Chicago Business as a Notable Leader in HR in 2020, by ALPFA as one of the Most Powerful Latinas in 2019, and by the International Association of Business Communicators. She is a graduate of Calumet College of St. Joseph and DePaul University's Kellstadt Graduate School of Business. She also serves on the board of directors of several not-for-profit organizations.

In her free time, Vicki enjoys reading, learning, decorating, playing with her four grandchildren and joining her husband on his never-ending adventures.

You can learn more about Vicki at vickiznavor.com.

Use the next few pages for keeping ing specific notes and references.

YOUR NOTES

ENDNOTES

1   Steve Jobs, "Steve Jobs' 2005 Stanford Commencement Address," https://www.youtube.com/watch?v=Hd_ptbiPoXM

2   Brent Schlender and Rick Tetzeli, *Becoming Steve Jobs* (New York: Crown Business, 2015)

3   Melanie Curtin, "25 Oprah Winfrey Quotes That Will Empower You (and Make You Laugh)," *Inc.*, February 11, 2019, https://www.inc.com/melanie-curtin/25-oprah-winfrey-quotes-that-will-empower-you-and-make-you-laugh.html

4   Balázs Kovács, "Authenticity Is in the Eye of the Beholder: The Exploration of Audiences" Lay Associations to Authenticity Across Five Domains," *Review of General Psychology* 23, no. 1 (March 2019): 32–59. https://doi.org/10.1177/1089268019829469.

5   David Viscott, *Finding Your Strength in Difficult Times* (New York: McGraw-Hill, 1993).

6   Nora Zamichow, "The David Viscott You Didn't Know," *Los Angeles Times,* January 26, 1997, https://www.latimes.com/archives/la-xpm-1997-01-26-tm-22135-story.html.

7   *"Top 20 Quotes of Ursula Burns,"* https://youtu.be/Io6TCAN2W38

8   Kovács, "Authenticity."

9   Carla A. Harris, *Expect to Win* (New York: Avery, 2009)

10   Grace Rivera, Andrew Christy, Jinhyung Kim, Matthew Vess, Joshua Hicks, and Rebecca Schlegel, "Understanding the Relationship Between Perceived Authenticity and Well-Being," *Review of General Psychology* 23, no. 1 (March 2019): 113–26, https://doi.org/10.1037/gpr0000161.

11   Serena Chen, "Authenticity in Context: Being True to Working Selves," *Review of General Psychology* 23, no. 1 (March 2019): 60–72, https://doi.org/10.1037/gpr0000160.

12   Roy Baumeister, "Stalking the True Self Through the Jungles of Authenticity: Problems, Contradictions, Inconsistencies, Disturbing Findings—and a Possible Way Forward," *Review of General Psychology* 23, no. 1 (March 2019): 143–54, https://doi.org/10.1177/1089268019829472.

13   Reba McEntire, https://www.goodreads.com/quotes/132414-to-succeed-in-life-you-need-three-things-a-wishbone

14   Katrina Jongman-Sereno and Mark Leary, "The Enigma of Being Yourself: A Critical Examination of the Concept of Authenticity," *Review of General Psychology* 23, no. 1 (March 2019): 133–42, https://doi.org/10.1037/gpr0000157.

15   Baumeister, "Stalking."

16   Rachel Chang, "16 Rosa Parks Quotes About Civil Rights," *Biography*, January 29, 2020, https://www.biography.com/news/rosa-parks-quotes

17   Jongman-Sereno and Leary, "Enigma."

18   William Fleeson and Joshua Wilt, "The Relevance of Big Five Trait Content in Behavior to Subjective Authenticity: Do High Levels of Within-Personality Variability Undermine or Enable Authenticity Achievement?" *Journal of Personality* 78, no. 4 (July 5, 2010): 1353–82, https://doi.org/10.1111/j.1467-6494.2010.00653.x.

19   "Tom Magliozzi Obituary," Car Talk, accessed July 10, 2020, https://www.cartalk.com/content/tom-magliozzi-obituary.

20   Sara Gaynes Levy, "Can You Really Be Yourself at Work?," *O, The Oprah Magazine,* May 15, 2019, https://www.oprahmag.com/life/work-money/a27457513/can-you-really-be-yourself-at-work/.

21   "Tina Opie" Babson College Faculty Profiles, accessed July 10, 2020, https://www.babson.edu/academics/faculty/faculty-profiles/tina-opie.php.

22   Alexajobs.com, "30 Inspirational Career Quotes," *Medium*, February 24, 2016. https://medium.com/career-relaunch/30-inspirational-career-quotes-2c26662adb99

23   Stephen Joseph, *Authentic: How to Be Yourself and Why It Matters* (London: Piatkus, Little, Brown Book Group, 2016).

24   Karen Salmansohn, Goodreads, https://www.goodreads.com/quotes/6891988-when-you-realize-how-much-you-re-worth-you-ll-stop-giving

25   John Maxwell Company, *"The Law of Awareness: 4 Questions to Help You Know Yourself,"* April 8, 2013, https://www.johnmaxwell.com/blog/the-law-of-awareness-4-questions-to-help-you-know-yourself/

26   Tasha Eurich, "Increase Your Self-Awareness with One Simple Fix," TEDx Talks, December 19, 2017, https://www.youtube.com/watch?v=tGdsOXZpyWE.

27   Amy Poehler, "You Can't Do It Alone," *Harvard Magazine,* May 25, 2011, https://harvardmagazine.com/2011/05/you-cant-do-it-alone

28   Michelle Sales, "5 Things You Can Learn from Brené Brown on Being a Better Leader," *Venture Magazine,* July 2020, https://www.theventuremag.com/connection-brene-brown/.

29   William Arruda, "How to Succeed by Being Your True Self at Work," *Forbes,* November 3, 2019, https://www.forbes.com/sites/williamarruda/2019/11/03/how-to-succeed-by-being-your-true-self-at-work/#d7eb4637f86f.

30   Joseph, *Authentic.*

31   Adam Hickman and Jennifer Robison, "5 Facts About Engagement and Remote Workers," Gallup, May 1, 2020, https://www.gallup.com/workplace/309521/facts-engagement-remote-workers.aspx.

32   Goodreads.com, 2020.

33   Raymond Trau, Jane O'Leary, and Cathy Brown, "7 Myths About Coming Out at Work," *Harvard Business Review,* October 19, 2018, https://hbr.org/2018/10/7-myths-about-coming-out-at-work.

34   Katherine W. Phillips, Tracy L. Dumas, and Nancy P. Rothbard, "Diversity and Authenticity," *Harvard Business Review,* March/April 2018, https://hbr.org/2018/03/diversity-and-authenticity.

35   Mick Mooney, "The Price of Authenticity in Work and Life," *Mick Mooney* (blog), accessed July 10, 2020, https://www.mickmooney.com/blog/the-price-of-authenticity-in-work-life.

36   Rivera et al, "Understanding."

37   Amy Bucher, "Authenticity as a Path to Happiness," *Amy Bucher* (blog), July 16, 2014, https://www.amybucherphd.com/authenticity-as-a-path-to-happiness/.

38   Jessica Simpson, Open Book (New York: Dey Street Books, 2020)

39   Brian Floriani, "What Is the Difference between Success and Significance?" TEDx Talks, September 2, 2016, https://www.youtube.com/watch?v=oW5BOSl0RQ0

40   *"Best Jennifer Lopez Quotes About Life That'll Surprise You,"* Stackliving, July 18, 2020, https://www.stackliving.com/quotes/jennifer-lopez-quotes/

41   Kirsten Weir, "Feel Like a Fraud?," *American Psychological Association,* accessed July 10, 2020, https://www.apa.org/gradpsych/2013/11/fraud.

42 Bruce L. Katcher, "Employees Are Afraid to Speak Up," *Discovery Surveys,* accessed July 10, 2020, http://www.discoverysurveys.com/articles/itw-014.html.

43 Jay Steinfeld, "5 Reasons Why Employees Don't Speak Up and How to Fix It," *Inc.,* August 10, 2017, https://www.inc.com/jay-steinfeld/5-reasons-why-employees-dont-speak-up-and-6-ways-t.html.

44 Martin Luther King, Jr. https://www.goodreads.com/quotes/11236-in-the-end-we-will-remember-not-the-words-of

45 Elizabeth Segran, "How Hiding Your True Self at Work Can Hurt Your Career," *Fast Company,* September 17, 2015, https://www.fastcompany.com/3051111/how-hiding-your-true-self-at-work-can-hurt-your-career#https%3A%2F%2Fwww.fastcompany.com%3A443.

46 Kenji Yoshino, *Covering: The Hidden Assault on Our Civil Rights* (New York: Random House, 2007).

47 Sims Wyeth, "17 Inspiring Quotes to Help You Face Your Fears," *Inc.*, October 10, 2014, https://www.inc.com/sims-wyeth/17-inspiring-quotes-to-help-you-face-your-fears.html

48 Jack Canfield, *The Success Principles* (New York: HarperCollins, 2005).

49 Mike Robbins, *Be Yourself, Everyone Else Is Already Taken* (San Francisco: Jossey-Bass, 2009).

50 Sims Wyeth, "17 Inspiring Quotes to Help You Face Your Fears," *Inc.*, October 10, 2014, https://www.inc.com/sims-wyeth/17-inspiring-quotes-to-help-you-face-your-fears.html

51 Robbins, *Be Yourself.*

52 Mike Jaffe, *Wake Up! Your Life Is Calling* (Bloomington, IN: AuthorHouse, 2011).

53 Maya Angelou, Facebook, March 4, 2020, https://www.facebook.com/MayaAngelou/posts/try-to-live-your-life-in-a-way-that-you-will-not-regret-years-of-useless-virtue-/10159020724199796/.

54   Tinybuddha.com

55   "Speaking with Authenticity: Know Your Audience, Tell Your Story,"
     Sierra Leadership, accessed July 10, 2020, https://sierraleadership.
     com/2017/07/30/authentic-speaking-audience/.

56   Goodreads.com

57   Lisa Rosh and Lynn Offermann, "Be Yourself, But Carefully," *Harvard
     Business Review,* October 2013, https://hbr.org/2013/10/be-your-
     self-but-carefully.

58   Mark Travers, "The Truth About Gossip," *Psychology Today,* May 14, 2019,
     https://www.psychologytoday.com/us/blog/social-instincts/201905/
     the-truth-about-gossip.

59   Judith Humphrey, "Emotionally Intelligent Ways to Express These 5
     Feelings at Work," *Fast Company,* February 17, 2018, https://www.fast-
     company.com/40529677/emotionally-intelligent-ways-to-express-these-
     5-feelings-at-work.

60   Canfield, Success Principles.

61   https://www.etymonline.com/word/conflict

62   Jennifer Goldman-Wetzler, PhD, *Optimal Outcomes: Free Yourself
     From Confict At Work, At Home, And In Life* (New York: HarperCollins
     Publish-ers Inc., 2020).

63   Lin-Manuel Miranda and Jeremy McCarter, *Hamilton: The Revolution* (New
     York: Grand Central Publishing, 2016).

64   Joan Podrazik, "Oprah's Life Lesson from Maya Angelou:
     When People Show You Who They Are, Believe Them," *HuffPost,*
     March 14, 2013, https://www.huffpost.com/entry/oprah-life-
     lesson-maya-an-gelou_n_2869235

65   Kenneth Cloke and Joan Goldsmith, *Resolving Conflicts at Work: Ten Strategies for Everyone on the Job* (San Francisco: Jossey-Bass, 2000, 2005, 2011).

66   Cloke and Goldsmith, *Resolving Conflicts at Work*.

67   Randal Gilmore, *Overcome Conflict Through the Power of Samemindedness: 7 Disciplines and a Proven Process to Achieve Genuine Agreement* (EXALT Publications, 2018).

68   Valerie Berset-Price, "Courage at Work: Why Removing the Fear Barrier Increases Cross-Cultural Corporate Success," *HuffPost*, April 15, 2016, https://www.huffpost.com/entry/courage-at-work-why-remov_b_9702034

69   Goodreads.com. 2020.

70   Ellie Ballentine, "Wonder, Curiosity and Openness," *Ellie Ballentine: The Mindset Mentor*, https://ellieballentine.com/mindset-wisdom-tip/curiosity/,

71   Brené Brown, *Rising Strong: How the Ability to Reset Transforms The Way We Live, Love, Parent, and Lead* (New York: Random House, 2015).

72   Rasmus Hougaard, "Four Reasons Why Compassion Is Better for Humanity Than Empathy," *Forbes,* July 8, 2020, https://www.forbes.com/sites/rasmushougaard/2020/07/08/four-reasons-why-compassion-is-better-for-humanity-than-empathy/#6cbd3b41d6f9

73   "The Power of Forgiveness," *Harvard Health Publishing,* May 2019, https://www.health.harvard.edu/mind-and-mood/the-power-of-forgiveness

74   Randy Kamen, "The Power of Forgiveness," *HuffPost,* October 26, 2012, https://www.huffpost.com/entry/forgiveness_b_2006882

75   Evan Carmichael, "Oprah Winfrey Motivation - Best Interview Moments," December 10, 2016. https://www.youtube.com/watch?v=T-T0DOvnx0Oc&feature=share

76   David Viscott, *Finding Your Strength in Difficult Times* (New York: McGraw-Hill, 1993).

77   Josh A. Dykstra, "A Tale of Three Bricklayers," October 27, 2011, https://joshallan.com/2011/10/17/a-tale-of-three-bricklayers/

78   David Viscott, *Finding Your Strength in Difficult Times* (New York: McGraw-Hill, 1993).

79   McDowell, Emily. (2020). Retrieved from https://emilymcdowell.com/products/finding-yourself-card

80   Kate Bowler, "Emily McDowell: There's No Good Card for That," Everything Happens: A Podcast with Kate Bowler, https://katebowler.com/podcasts/emily-mcdowell-theres-no-good-card-for-that-s2e1/

81   Kate Bowler, "Everything Happens for a Reason and Other Lies I've Loved," July 2, 2019, https://www.youtube.com/watch?v=DTc-JmIbn5nw.

82   "Oprah 5 Moments That Changed My Life," *Pressreader,* October 28, 2019, https://www.pressreader.com/australia/who/20191028/281633897004672

83   Jen Sincero, *You Are a Badass: How to Stop Doubting Your Greatness and Start Living An Awesome Life* (Philadelphia: Running Press, 2013).

84   Aaron McHugh, Fire Your Boss: Discover Work You Love Without Quitting Your Job (New York: Post Hill Press, 2020).

85   Oprah Winfrey, "Oprah and Alicia Keys: The Interview," Oprah's Super-Soul Conversations, April 1, 2020. https://open.spotify.com/episode/0QIOdehSMu10ZwJR11BfEV?si=iPwfFGRRQT2IFZ3oRTf8Ow

86   Oprah Winfrey, "Life First Speaks to You in a Whisper," Oprah's SuperSoul Conversations, July 22, 2020. https://open.spotify.com/

episode/3U35MSLagg0CMJhUHFTXOF?si=FVITMetTTnuntTUc-0QXL0w

87   Deepak Chopra, *Spiritual Solutions: Answers to Life's Greatest Challenges* (New York: Harmony Books, 2012), Kindle.

88   "Top 10 Reasons Employees Stay with an Organization," CAI Empowering Employees, September 22, 2017, https://www.capital.org/s/content/a0Y410000058F6nEAE/blogtop-10-reasons-employees-stay-with-an-organization

89   Monica Torres, "12 People Share Why They Quit Their Jobs," *Huff-Post*, April 30, 2019, https://www.huffpost.com/entry/why-people-quit-jobs_l_5cc71110e4b08e4e348584f0

90   Mia Shabsove," 10 Clear Signs You Should Stay at Your Job or Leave ASAP," Narcity, 2018, https://www.narcity.com/life/10-clear-signs-you-should-stay-at-your-job-or-leave-asap

91   Monique Valcour, "When Burnout Is a Sign You Should Leave Your Job," *Harvard Business Review*, January 25, 2018, https://hbr.org/2018/01/when-burnout-is-a-sign-you-should-leave-your-job

92   Shelcy V. Joseph, "Should You Stay At Your Current Job?" *Forbes*, December 7, 2019, https://www.forbes.com/sites/shelcyvjoseph/2019/12/07/should-you-stay-at-your-current-job/#701039c72f27

93   Thomas Heath, "How to Quit a Job You Hate with Grace," *Washington Post*, January 4, 2017, https://www.washingtonpost.com/news/business/wp/2017/01/04/how-to-quit-a-job-you-hate-with-grace/

94   Retrieved from Goodreads.com

95   Anna Black, *A Year of Living Mindfully: Week-by-Week Mindfulness Meditations for a More Contented and Fulfilled Life* (New York: CICO Books, 2015).

96   Aida Muluneh, "The Wolf You Feed," https://www.aidamuluneh.com/

97   Wayne Dyer, "What Is The Ego?" July 1, 2014, https://youtu.be/p2Ly1D-b51Y

98   Deepak Chopra, *The Seven Spiritual Laws of Success: A Practical Guide to the Fulfillment of Your Dreams* (San Rafael, California: Amber-Allen Publishing, 1994).

99   Goodreads.com

100   Nancy Meyers, *The Holiday* (Columbia Pictures, Universal Pictures, Relativity Media, Waverly FIlms), 2006.

101   David Viscott, *Finding Your Strength in Difficult Times* (New York: McGraw-Hill, 1993).

Made in the USA
Coppell, TX
27 June 2022